Scandalous Space

Between architecture and archaeology

Alessandro Zambelli

Contents

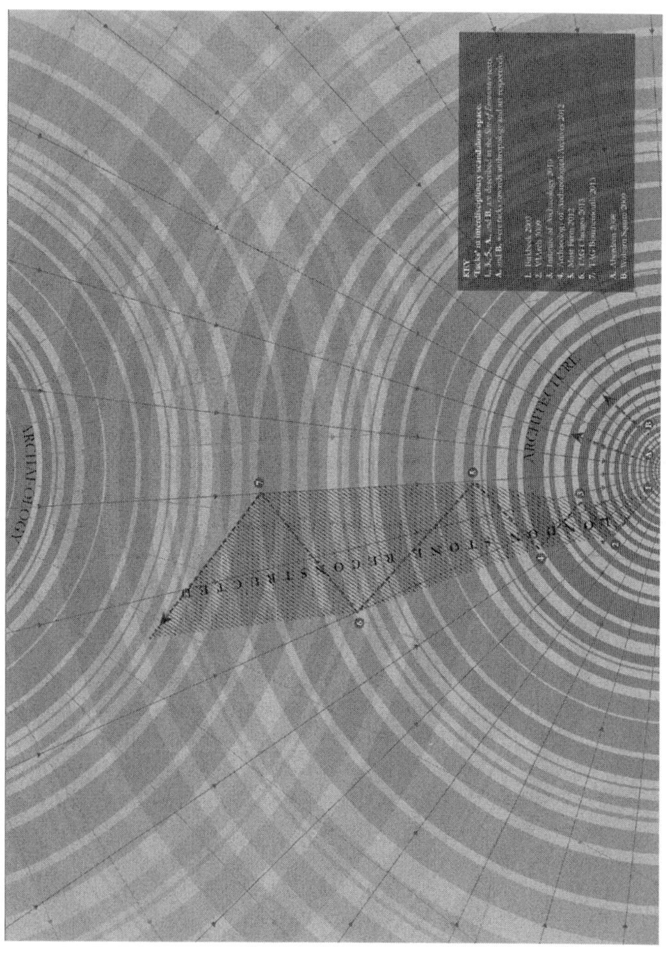

Fig. 1 Alessandro Zambelli, Chart of the Scandalous Space Between Architecture and Archaeology.

Introduction

As the fifteenth-century Kentish rebel Jack Cade struck London Stone, he pronounced himself transformed into Lord Mortimer and Lord of the City of London (Cade was not related to Richard Duke of York as the surname 'Mortimer' would, then, have implied, there is substantial doubt that his name was even, in fact, Cade). As he struck the Stone he decreed also that "piss" running in the public gutters be transmuted into wine. Five hundred and seventy years later a fragment of the Stone remains on Cannon Street not far from, but not exactly, where Cade struck it.[1]

Later, William Shakespeare was quite clear that Cade's power to turn the world upside down was ratified in the striking with his staff of this, London's fetish stone, its protective palladium. The Stone itself bears witness to and so validates the transubstantiations wrought through Cade's revolt: foot soldier to Lord; rural naïf to urban adept; water to wine. Cade's transgression of social and physical categories recalls the story of Christ's miraculous transformation of water to wine, but Shakespeare's Cade is a bathetic rather than a transcendent figure and under his stewardship these alchemic transformations stem from baser material, even, than everyday water. At the end of the fifteenth-century claret was not, as it later became, a synonym for red wine from Bordeaux, instead it qualified the colour of the wine; somewhere between red and white, and not exactly rosé either. And, of course, claret has also come to stand in for blood. Four hundred and fifty-one years later Rebecca Daisy who had, for eighteen years, kept a "sweetstuff stall" next to London Stone protested, when asked to move on from her pitch, that "she [would] go quietly" only when she was "removed in a narrow box."[2] This overthrow of social order – and the 'spilling of a little claret' – is rife with transgression, with slippage; Cade, like Mrs. Daisy, was no blue blood but neither was he quite, any more, a commoner – as he struck London Stone he and his staff became something in-between; Cade, a scandalous practitioner of his own new Law and his staff, an instrument instantly reforged through contact with London Stone, for the enforcement of that Law. We will return to the adventures of Jack and Rebecca in the final two chapters of this book.

London Stone is an artefact of oolitic limestone whose manufacture may date from Roman times.[3] And yet it is scarcely an 'archaeological' artefact at all, since almost no work of that category has ever been done upon it, set adrift, as it has been, from its ancient physical contexts. Indeed, the work that has been done in connection with the Stone which most closely approximates archaeological practice is much more like what might be categorised as historical practice. E. H. Carr would have seen this as a positive attribute, for him, "archaeology, epigraphy, numismatics, chronology" are mere "'auxiliary' sciences of history."[4] Africanist historian and anthropologist Jan Vansina more conventionally characterises the differences thus, "most historians deal with written or oral messages. Most archaeological findings document situations, while historians often focus on sources which document events."[5] Those that have attempted to describe London Stone have tended to treat it as if it were such an "event," a prolonged event recorded in words and sometimes in drawings or photographs, but always tied to London around it, both physically through its ever-eroding presence and through complex, as I shall go on to describe, networks of analogical connectivity.

Such is the transformative power of analogy; its unique ability to carry meaning, anaphorically, across fields of knowledge and, for the purposes of this account, *disciplinary* fields, forging, "the most beautiful bond possible" the bond of analogy.[6] The logic and the sympathetic magic of analogy underpin the arguments of this book just as it underpins the interdisciplinary structures it describes and employs. Throughout, I will describe experimental practices performed in the space provided by these analogical networks. Working, in particular, directly upon London Stone, using it as a common locus for the interconnected disciplines of architecture and archaeology as revealed through their shared drawing practices – disciplines which have, in various ways, claimed the Stone as their own.

> *I suppose, architects and archaeologists could be regarded as procedurally equal but temporally opposed: after all the very same tool – the trowel – that the builder uses to fabricate the architectural forms of the future is used by the archaeologist, in the excavation of a site, to reveal the forms of the past.*[7]

What are archaeologists and architects doing, and what do they believe they are doing, when they pick up a pen or pencil, or when they open a piece of C.A.D. software (we will come to trowels in Sites of Encounter: Must Farm below)? What do their respective disciplines purport to be doing when their practitioners employ drawing practices? Do architects and archaeologists draw differently and do the instrumentalities implicit in their drawings stand opposed to one another as is often casually assumed – one future-facing and the other orientated towards the past? Tim Ingold, in the quotation above, illustrates one way of thinking about the tangled relationship of architecture and archaeology, relationships which this book aims to demonstrate and explain, even as it uses those knotted connections to make interdisciplinary work between them. In fact, I aim to show that architecture and archaeology are not at all "procedurally equal," but that they share a more nuanced relationship of procedural resemblance, and that, even more emphatically, they do not stand "temporally opposed."

The relationship of archaeology to that other purportedly past-facing discipline, history, provides evidence of the dangers of assuming, or seeking, direct connections to the past. In historiography, superficially at least, the dangers of this view do seem to have been understood. In 1995 writing of the mid-twentieth-century Annales School, Aron Gurevich observed that;

> *the historians of a new cast are very far from the old illusion of being able to 'resurrect' the past, to 'live themselves into it' and to demonstrate it 'wie es eigentlich gewesen war'. They clearly understood that historical reconstruction is no more and no less than construction, that the historian's role is incomparably more active and creative than their predecessors believed."*[8]

"Wie es eigentlich gewesen" is usually translated as "how things actually were," an influential principle in the rise of source-based history from Leopold von Ranke's 1824 work, *Geschichte der romanischen und germanischen Völker*.[9] By going to primary sources, sources often personal and only obliquely related to the main subjects of mainstream histories, von Ranke's idea was that a closer approximation, a more accurate reconstruction, of historical cultures could be made. Tod Presner describes this account of the relationship between event and narrative as demanding, "a structural homology between real events and the narrative strategies used to represent, capture, and render them meaningful."[10] For von Ranke and his followers the past was, through these empirical reconstructions, solved or at least rendered solvable. Walter Benjamin like Gurevich, was unconvinced, and described von Ranke's "wie es eigentlich gewesen" as, "the strongest narcotic of the [nineteenth] century."[11] By the time E. H. Carr wrote in his influential *What is History* in 1961 that, "by and large, the historian will get the kind of facts he wants. History means interpretation"[12] interpretive and reflexive historiographies had already marginalised empirical reconstructions understood, as they were, to be part of this now discredited empiricist historiography. Following suit, archaeology became freer, it seemed, to make reconstructions through multivalent, reflexive interpretations of hitherto mainstream archaeological evidence.[13] Work at, for example, Çatalhöyük[14] in Turkey or the explicitly titled *Cotúa Island-Orinoco Reflexive Archaeology Project*[15] have now established a kind of archaeology without (professional) archaeologists in the spirit, perhaps, of Bernard Rudofsky's *Architecture Without Architects*[16] though shorn of architecture's alternative central tradition of the vernacular. Where Rudofsky's "non-pedigree" architect might tap into ancient local practices of building, no equivalent tradition is available to an archaeologist. Instead, as I will argue, architecture as an overtly design-based discipline can lend to archaeology ways of re-casting its own reconstructive practices to reveal forms of propositional making already latent within them. Chapter 2 will examine in detail the kind of making characterised by its 'propositional' nature – propositional that is in the sense derived from Bruno Latour's "proposition" which, "designates a certain way of loading an entity into another by making the second attentive to the first, and by making both of them diverge from their usual path, their usual interpretation."[17]

It has been argued that archaeology is like architecture in reverse.[18] If architecture looks to the future by making drawn propositions then archaeology designs also, but in the form of reconstructions of the past. This book argues further that design and reconstruction are simultaneously central to both disciplines and are forms of propositional making; archaeologists have no direct access to the past and so their reconstructions are compelled to be propositional, and that equally, architectural propositions are reconstructive. As Nicholas Stanley-Price has put it, "a reconstructed building – if based primarily on excavated evidence – must be considered a new building (reconstruction as a creative act)."[19] Archaeology reveals for architecture a form of making based on practice whose connection to the past is not, as with architecture, predicated on quasi-mysterious, and in any case contested, canons of ancient form-making and monographic histories, but which makes available both evidence-based and interpretive practices (for example; particular excavation techniques, assemblage, finds interpretation, all of which will be discussed in more detail below). But the reliance of mainstream archaeology upon, in particular, empirical evidence to the exclusion of more speculative reconstructive design, should not replace the playfulness central to conventional design disciplines. Because for archaeology, architecture in its turn can reveal precisely that invention and speculative engagement with, often, ambiguous or contradictory evidence (for example; site, programme, technology) which defines and provokes the design practice latent within it. Writing more generally of interpretation within archaeological practice rather than reconstruction itself (which often follows in short order) Jean Gero claims that, "the practice of archaeology over-emphasizes and over-rewards unambiguous certainty in our interpretations, even though our conclusions are usually drawn from necessarily partial, underdetermined and complex evidence."[20]

These disciplinary inversions make available to archaeology, but also to architecture, a shift in understanding of what a reconstruction or a design might be for – what it is capable of doing. What for the architect are fragments of brief (proposals from a client for a building), context (the physical, historical, political and economic environment from which a design and any subsequent building might emerge) and tectonics (the way a design and any subsequent building might be thoughtfully put together), for the archaeologist are analogous fragments of evidence. And although it is something of a truism that the collection and use of these fragments for the archaeologist faces the past (what did the building look like to which these fragments belonged?) and for the architect faces the future (what will the building look like to which these fragments belong?), I would argue that this has little effect other than to occlude the over-arching propositional character of both design and reconstruction. That is, at the moment of enquiry – in the present – there is no building, but the design, just like the reconstruction, proposes one.

To emphasise this point I quote below at length from Kevin Greene's standard archaeological primer *Archaeology: An Introduction*. The practices described in this text are not similar to descriptions of architectural practices, they are, but for the words "excavation," "interpretation" and, of course, "reconstruction," identical;

> *An excellent way of increasing understanding of an excavated building is to create a scale model or reconstruction drawing. [...] Fragments of architectural stonework such as window or door frames, voussoirs from arches and vaulting, and roofing slates and tiles, all may help to date the building as well as to reconstruct it [...] Excavators also benefit from the detailed analysis of the excavated remains; new interpretations may be suggested, and attention drawn to parts of a site that need further investigation. If several plausible reconstructions are deduced from a single plan it is best to offer more than one interpretation in an excavation report. Computer graphics are now very sophisticated, and virtual reality modelling (VRM) of structures allows viewers to look around the interior, or inspect the appearance of the exterior from any angle.*[21]

As I will argue later, amongst those disciplines which define themselves, at least in part, by the production, or design, of objects and collections of objects, we can see various structures or models of making develop over time. These paradigms of making, often in normative, institutionally directed ways, but also in transgressive modes, help to define and in some cases police the centres of their discipline, or blur them respectively. The transdisciplinary move across the space between such centres towards other disciplines is, in this account, described as *scandalous*. The notion of the scandal will be used as shorthand for the processes of archaeological-architectural interdisciplinarity[22] following an outline below, of the origins of the term in Claude Lévi-Strauss's *The Elementary Structures of Kinship*.[23] In this view, the scandal provides a framework for understanding resemblances between homologous disciplines and, I argue, between architecture and, through antiquarianism, archaeology in particular. It also describes more precisely the kind of interdisciplinarity necessary for the type of transgressive practice central to this book. So, although Lévi-Strauss, uncontroversially, considers the natural and the cultural to be mutually exclusive and exhaustive sets of social practices, rare conditions which do conform to both – for example the incest taboo – catalyse, for him, a kind of cross-practice scandal.

In this book, analogy is adopted as a method of transgressive, visual practice. This practice functions because, as I will argue, a homological relationship exists between some disciplines, in this case architecture and archaeology, a homology which, founded upon common suites of tools and techniques has been occluded, and is rediscovered through the intimately related practices of design and reconstruction. This is a mode of interdisciplinarity which manifests itself in categories of drawing and recording interrogated, and sometimes modified, to reveal processes, in archaeology, more commonly associated with design, and processes, in architecture, more commonly associated with reconstruction. In order to produce work between these different practices of making, new or, the retrieving of old, sometimes obsolete or abandoned, undisciplined tools and techniques is required. These are further developed and employed below in Chapter 2. London Stone Reconstructed.

How are we to characterise the tools and techniques which function within what I argue is the analogical, navigable, space between architecture and archaeology? What form of practice is it possible to sustain at this intersection? And crucially, what is to be gained from practising there? It is within this *scandalous space* that I seek to answer these questions and to posit a role for this kind of practice in relation to its parent disciplines. Between design and reconstruction and between architecture and archaeology, therefore lies a scandalous space for transgressive practice where scandalous artefacts may be made.

Site of Encounter

Birkbeck

In 1967, Robert Smithson wrote that in the everyday industrial and commercial "monuments" of suburban New York he was witnessing, "ruins in reverse." That, "the buildings don't fall into ruin after they are built but rather rise into ruin before they are built."[24] This observation has, over the years, struck a chord with architects and archaeologists alike.[25] In particular I was reminded of a sketch I had made early in the researching of this book, no more than a doodle really – a sketch reproduced here in Figure 2.[26] It implies, at first glance, a clockwise circularity of architectural and archaeological processes; empty plot, to scaffolded construction, to completed building, to extendedbuilding, eventually to ruin, and so to excavated archaeological site. And then it seemed to me that this circularity might, with a little imagination, be productively

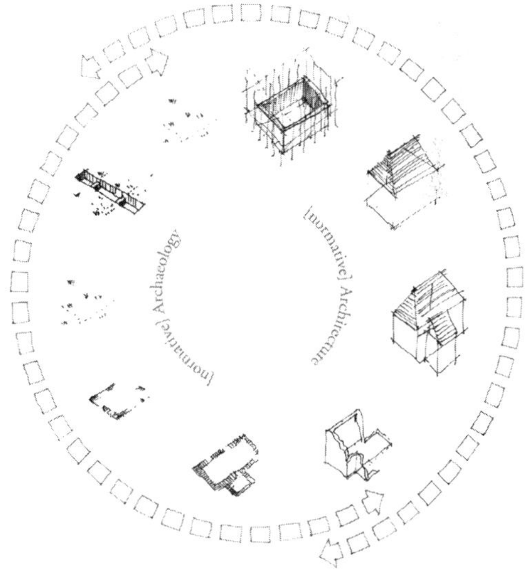

Fig. 2 Alessandro Zambelli, The Circularity of Architectural and Archaeological Processes. 2018.

undermined, that it could be read instead as; empty plot, to a sequence of ruins rising towards ever more complete states – as one might build a folly, to a building scaffolded for demolition, then to its site excavated to reveal earlier buried forms of itself.

The inversion is imperfect, yet revealed for me an uncanny mirroring of normative disciplinary processes – an uncanniness I will return to below. Smithson observes of one of Passaic's "timeless" voids, "that monumental parking lot divided the city in half, turning it into a mirror and a reflection – but the mirror kept changing places with the reflection. One never knew what side of the mirror one was on."[27] But architecture and archaeology are not only, or not simply, "reversals" of one another, they are situated reversals – places where design and reconstruction meet, where construction and ruin encounter one another. This "site of encounter"[28] and the one at Must Farm at the end of this book are analogical sites, but they are also physical places in space and time occupied by people practicing in a variety of interdisciplinary forms. Figure 1 characterises these sites[29] as places and moments where my interdisciplinary practice has 'tacked' in order to navigate across disciplinary ripples towards archaeology. Site of Encounter: Birkbeck and Site of Encounter: Must Farm are brief descriptions of this transdisciplinary tacking.

In 2003, in order to satisfy a long-standing, yet at that time casual, interest in archaeology I enrolled on an evening course at Birkbeck, University of London. This short course was part of their certificate in the Archaeology of the Palaeolithic and Mesolithic Periods.[30] Although run by Birkbeck, the sessions were hosted by the U.C.L. Institute of Archaeology three hundred meters away to the north housed in a building founded by Tessa and Mortimer Wheeler in 1937 and to which it moved in 1958.[31] Birkbeck, itself established in 1823 as the London Mechanics' Institute, was founded for the education of working adults and, because this was still its principal function in 2003, I was able to attend whilst simultaneously running my architectural practice.[32] *I was not particularly interested in acquiring an archaeology qualification, my intention at that time was simply to understand the subject in a little more detail – something to take me 'out' of architecture, briefly, once a week.*

As the course progressed, however, I became aware of a growing sense of familiarity with some of the materials we were using and with the techniques we were being asked to employ. Norah Moloney, who ran the evening class, is a specialist in lithic analysis[33] *and the room we used at the Institute also contained collections of lithic artefacts. In particular I remember two kinds of drawing which Norah asked us to tackle. The first were those, by others, in text books which we had been encouraged to refer to; sectional reconstructions of early buildings – drawings which seemed to me curiously like 'planning stage' architectural drawings. That is, scaled drawings containing just enough informationto be structurally and constructionally plausible and which often form the basis of applications for building licences from local government authorities in the U.K.*

The second, and more important, were drawings – rapid sketches really – that we, as a class, were asked to prepare of some of the stone tools available in the room. Figure 3 is an example of one such sketch, the making of which, as I will explain below, proved to be an uncannily familiar and, in a (very) small way, a memorably transgressive act.

That 'uncanniness' brings to mind, now, Sigmund Freud's re-working and expansion of Ernst Jentsch's 1906 work On The Psychology Of The Uncanny *in his own essay of 1919.*[34] *Freud agreed with Jentsch that certain uncomfortable, even frightening feelings of displacement, commonly described in remarkably similar terms across a number of European cultures and languages, could be defined most completely in the German word heimlich. And that;*

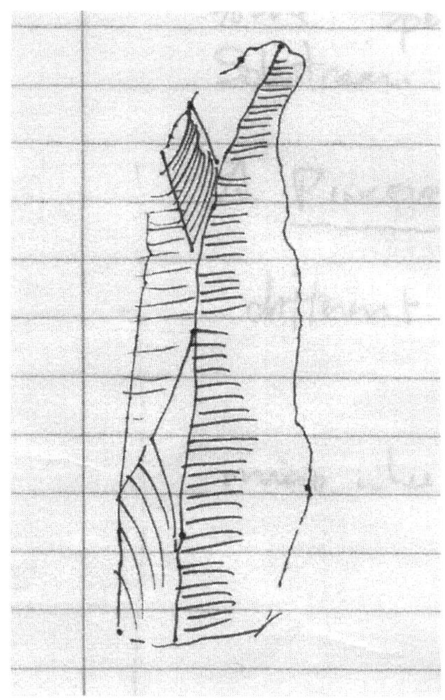

Fig.3 Alessandro Zambelli, Sketch of a Flint Burin, 2003.

> among its different shades of meaning the word 'heimlich' exhibits one which is identical with its opposite, 'unheimlich'. What is heimlich thus comes to be unheimlich.[35]

Heimlich and unheimlich both mean that, "what is familiar and agreeable," but also, "what is concealed and kept out of sight"[36] *are simultaneously true. Freud continues;*

> Schelling says something which throws quite a new light on the concept of the Unheimlich, for which we were certainly not prepared. According to him, everything is

> unheimlich that ought to have remained secret and hidden but has come to light.[37]

To this we can add the uncanny apparition of the 'double'. Whilst drawing the stone tools it seemed to me as though I were seeing, or in some other way sensing (the practice of drawing it) doubled. The drawings I was making in this archaeology class became somehow uncoupled from both my discipline – architecture, and from the discipline towards which I was working – archaeology. At first it seemed that this doubled act of drawing was both architecture and archaeology, *but I realised that it could not strictly be part of archaeology (I was not an archaeologist) but neither would the products of this hybrid practice be recognised by architects as architecture. These drawings belonged to neither discipline, yet were related to both.*

Unlike Freud who, in seeing himself reflected in the glass door of a train carriage failed to recognise this "inferior" and challenging double,[38] I have been seeking, through the making of this book, to understand the source and possible uses of this doubling, the effect of, "meeting one's own image unbidden and unexpected."[39] This doubling, alongside the "repetition" Freud identified as underlying the unheimlich occurs, I maintain, because of the parallel development of architectural and archaeological practices and their interconnected origins.

Some years after this event I came across the following text which, for its uncanniness, is worth repeating at length;

> *There is need for some* degree of confidence if a good line is to be drawn exactly in the right place, but often the inexperienced draughtsman loses his nerve and judgment when confronted with an expensive and cleanly beautiful sheet of drawing-paper or linen.
>
> [...] a good word may be said, for mechanical pencils

such as the Mars 'Lumograph', which allow the lead to be extruded or retracted at will and have moderately efficient devices for producing a sharp point.

[...] if he wishes to learn his craft thoroughly he will be well advised to serve a period of apprenticeship to the old-fashioned, hand-dipped pen, which is still used by some of the most supremely accomplished technical draughtsmen of our time.

[...] it is of the utmost importance that every drawing should bear a drawn scale rather than a mere written note of the representative fraction.[40]

Somewhat like the text from Archaeology: An Introduction *quoted above this text sounded, at least to my disciplined, professionalised ears, as though it might be about the training of an architect; the terms used for drawing tools and techniques though somewhat outmoded, would be familiar to an architect of a certain age – to those generations of architects who learned in precisely this way, with these tools, and those like me who had trained in these skills though they were already dying. Yet this quotation comes from Brian Hope-Taylor's book called* Archaeological Draughtsmanship *– and it is about archaeological drawing practice. It was curiously unsettling to read this text for the first time – this was, after all, the secret knowledge of my profession, re-revealed to me, somewhat distorted, in a kind of undisciplinary mirror.*

Chapter 1

Reconstruction

Disciplinarities

The disciplinary move from architecture towards archaeology is a moment of dramatic rupture. Jane Rendell argues that working between disciplines demands that;

> *we exchange what we know for what we do not know, and that we give up the safety of competence and specialism for the fears of inability and failure, the experience of interdisciplinary work produces a potentially destabilizing engagement with existing power structures, allowing the emergence of fragile forms of untested knowledge and uncertain understanding.*[41]

This mode of interdisciplinary work is work at risk but which can at the same time be a profoundly productive practice inviting the participation of other disciplines. Hal Foster claims that, "to be interdisciplinary you need to be disciplinary first – to be grounded in one discipline, preferably two, to know the historicity of these discourses before you test them against each other."[42] This reads not unlike Donald Campbell's 1969 appeal against the perceived problem of multidisciplinary training, he wrote that, "too often in discussions of interdisciplinary training one hears calls for breadth, for comprehensiveness. Too often we attempt the production of multidisciplinary scholars, professionals who have mastered two or more disciplines, rather than interdisciplinary specialists."[43] In this plea for the systematic adoption of interdisciplinary studies, Campbell emphasises the essential apartness of groups of disciplines and calls for practice in the "interdisciplinary gaps" between them.[44] In terms of the nature and condition of the disciplinary clusters between which the new work was supposed to be done, Campbell's approach lacks disciplinary specificity. Except that is, for the almost axiomatic position taken at this time, that the disciplinary clusters would be sciences.[45] Instead, Campbell prefers a different model, referred to by him light-heartedly (though with serious intent) as the fish-scale model; a model where disciplines would form a contiguous, overlapping disciplinary skin. In fact, Campbell is at pains to point out that many of what were then considered to be discrete, monolithic disciplines, were in fact already "arbitrary composites;" anthropology, sociology, psychology, geography, political science and economics are all described, somewhat facetiously, as a "hodgepodge."[46]

Specific work on interdisciplinarity within design practice was not systematically attempted until Craig Bremner and Paul Rodgers *Design Without Discipline* in 2013,[47] an analysis itself built upon the work of John Chris Jones in 1992[48] and of Nigel Cross in 2006.[49] Campbell's study predates the seminal first international conference on interdisciplinarity held at the University of Nice in 1970,[50] so lacks what has become the, more or less, conventionalised terminology for such work. Nevertheless Campbell understands interdisciplinary work as an overlapping form of practice, where individual disciplines remain uncontaminated by one another. This model persisted into and beyond the accounts of interdisciplinarity of Julie Thompson Klein,[51] and Alex Coles and Alexia Defert,[52] all of which describe the tension implied in any interdisciplinary system, but not the demand for *movement* between or across disciplines. Nor do they describe what kinds of practice, or between which disciplines, these kinds of interdisciplinarity might occur. I argue that although it may be possible to do interdisciplinary work at the intersection of any two or more disciplines, this is not the case in the particular interdisciplinary space which I define in this account as scandalous. Here, there is no boundary overlap (there are, as I will also go on to argue, no such things as disciplinary boundaries), because overlap implies groundedness not only in one's own discipline but also in the 'other' discipline which any would-be interdisciplinary practitioner may not in fact have. Indeed, groundedness in one discipline, the practitioner's base discipline, but not the 'other' is essential because, using Lévi-Strauss's definition of scandal,[53] the hybrid practice must allow itself to be governed by the contingent rules of the base discipline; the architect practising scandalously, necessarily remains an architect.

Other critics have argued for a utopian site of interdisciplinary production – a site free from the hegemonic influences of normative disciplinarities. Elizabeth Grosz argues for just such a space; outside of both her discipline of philosophy and of the strictures of architecture, the discipline with which she would work;

> *To explore architecture philosophically would entail submitting architectural design, construction, and theory to the requirements and exigencies of philosophical discourse, the rigor of philosophical argument, and the abstraction of philosophical speculation. And to examine philosophy architecturally would require using philosophical concepts and propositions, wrenched from their own theoretical context and transformed, perhaps mutilated, for architectural purposes. In either case, one discipline would submit the other to its internal needs and constraints, reducing it to its subordinated other.*[54]

I would argue that this "submission" is both inevitable and to be welcomed. If we accept Foster's claim that a pre-figuring disciplinary "groundedness" is necessary for interdisciplinary practice, then disciplinary hierarchy is unavoidable. But this submission is not orientated the way that Grosz thinks it is, nor is it an ungenerous relationship; this book describes the transdisciplinary movement away from architecture by an architect (me) and, at times, that architect's necessary submission to archaeology. In Latour's terms this is an "offer"[55] made by architecture to archaeology and a greater offer made by archaeology to architecture; I might offer the results of my practice at an archaeological conference, say, where "grounded" practitioners of archaeology might offer their, usually frank, views. The revised trajectory of this, now interdisciplinary, work may again be offered back to archaeology.

Grosz's answer to the problem of hierarchy is to posit the existence of a "third space" which she terms "the outside," a space which is external to the disciplines in question;

> *Outside each of the disciplines in their most privileged and accepted forms, outside the doxa and received conceptions, where they become experiment and innovation more than good sense with guaranteed outcomes, we will find the most perilous, experimental, and risky of texts and practices.*[56]

In this account of interdisciplinary, scandalous space Grosz's "third space" cannot exist; there is no "outside" to a discipline. The diagram in Figure 1 represents the transdisciplinary movements I have made from the strong "privileged" centre of architecture – from its professionalised heart – towards the somewhat less strong, somewhat less privileged (because that discipline is younger, less professionalised) discipline of archaeology. There are no boundaries *per se* around these – or any – disciplines, only ever-weakening ripples as the influence of particular disciplines recede infinitely across the space beyond their centres.

Foster's "testing" ground, therefore, is a very specific kind of arena available only to certain pre-defined participants which, for Julia Kristeva, is a "site of encounter."[57] Rendell describes it as a place "where individuals operate at the edge of, and between, disciplines," emphasising the "transformational experience" of this kind of practice and crucially, in situating interdisciplinarity within critical theory, she describes, in relation to the Hegelian dialectic, its "movement."[58]

Kristeva's interdisciplinary site of encounter is not simply a place of static proximity, rather, an "encounter" demands the kind of critical movement which Rendell describes and ascribes to the different category of the transdisciplinary. Rendell writes, "if interdisciplinarity is concerned with working in a place between disciplines in order to question their edges and borders, transdisciplinarity is often described as a horizontal movement, concerned with moving across disciplines, transversally."[59] It is worth noting that Rendell's understanding of the transdisciplinary is very different from that defined by Bremner and Rodgers and by Grosz for whom it means working across two or more disciplines with no 'base' discipline as such, "an understanding is demonstrated of at least two disciplinary competencies, neither of which is primary."[60] This book, because of the implicit 'movement' of the transdisciplinary, uses Rendell's definition.

So when Coles and Defert, for example, refer to

disciplinary "trajectories,"[61] and Klein emphasises its latent "productive" movement, writing that, "the relationship between disciplinarity and interdisciplinarity is not a paradox but a productive tension characterized by complexity and hybridity"[62] they are still referring to a kind of static interdisciplinarity where the move to that state of interdisciplinarity is somewhat taken for granted. But it is movement that provides the energy, or speed, to make trans, and thus interdisciplinary work. This movement and the speed required to make it is for Gilles Deleuze and Felix Guattari embodied in the figure of the "nomad" escaping the "state apparatus" as, "a movement [that] may be very fast, but that does not give it speed; a speed may be very slow, or even immobile, yet it is still speed. Movement is extensive; speed is intensive."[63] It is this paradoxical "immobile" "speed" which enables one, I argue, to lay down the pen or pencil in architecture and pick it up again a moment later in archaeology, never having left architecture. For Kristeva, this movement is one made in tandem between simultaneously practiced disciplines and involves, "the clear necessity to work disciplines differently but in parallel."[64]

Following Guattari's identification of "transversality" as a means for bypassing group hierarchies Rendell identifies this as a transdisciplinary movement at right-angles to disciplinary hierarchy; a confluence of forces which Kristeva describes simply as a "diagonal axis."[65] Guattari describes these kinds of indirect movement as;

> *opposed to: (a) verticality, as described in the organogramme of a pyramidal structure (leaders, assistants etc.); (b) horizontality, [...] a state of affairs in which things and people fit in as best they can with the situation in which they find themselves.*[66]

For Rendell this develops into the less geometrically prescriptive, more tactile notion, of the "cut on the bias."[67] The slip into terminology normally reserved for dressmaking implying a material manifestation of transdisciplinary forces – something to manipulate or that is available to make with. Again, Figure 1 describes the zigzag of the tack across disciplinary ripples made during and at the sites of encounter to be described in detail across the Sites of Encounter texts.

I would further argue that the transdisciplinary move into an interdisciplinary mode of practice always begins with a transgression; a transverse movement outward from a practice situated entirely within a practitioner's own "grounded" discipline and which explores beyond itself, tacking against the stratified flow of disciplinary hierarchies – the ripples of disciplinary influence – towards and through another, or many other, disciplines.

These sites of encounter and the transdisciplinary

navigation across them share striking similarities to Sarah Dillon's "palimpsestuous bodies." Dillon distinguishes between two types of analytical reading based on the palimpsest. A "palimpsestic" reading involves first separating the different layers of the palimpsest, an act which she says, "unravel[s] and destroy[s] the palimpsest."[68] A "palimpsestuous" reading, on the other hand, preserves the structure of the palimpsest and, "seeks to trace the incestuous and encrypted texts that constitute the palimpsest's fabric. Since those texts bear no necessary relation to each other, palimpsestuous reading is an inventive process of creating relations where there may, or should, be none; hence the appropriateness of its epithet's phonetic similarity to the incestuous."[69] A palimpsestuous reading requires making sense of a tangle of patterns in motion, and the analysis of contemporary culture is best accomplished by reading palimpsestuously; that is, by looking for and considering invented and imposed social relations that are otherwise hidden – that remain beneath the surface of the cultural text.

For Dillon, palimpsests "embody and provoke interdisciplinary encounter [...] admit[ing] all those terrains that write upon it to its body." Upon this body, "disciplines encounter each other [...] and their relationality becomes defined by its logic," engaging in a "productive violence of [...] involvement, entanglement, interruption and inhabitation of disciplines in and on each other."[70] This type of "inventive," creative reading; "the movement of elucidation,"[71] occurs upon the body of the palimpsest. In this account the act of tacking across these layers is an analogical, transdisciplinary move, and the "body" of the palimpsest, is a "site of encounter."[72] The space of this tacking movement is scandalous space and its navigation requires analogical techniques; techniques outlined in more detail below. Scandalous space allows something of Masaomi Kobayashi's definition of interdisciplinarity where he says that an interdisciplinary practitioner, "need[s] to be continuously situated in an in-between space, where they are conscious of both similarities and differences."[73] Though a helpful expansion of Foster's pre-disposing, disciplinary groundedness, this ignores the sense of direction implicit in Klein and Kristeva's accounts of interdisciplinarity, and made explicit in Rendell's account of transdisciplinarity. In addition, Kobayashi neglects the additional element of speed (or rather slowness) crucial to the formation of scandalous space. I argue that these slow, transverse, tacking actions are essential for achieving a kind of disciplinary escape velocity from disciplines and then for navigating through them towards others.

What kinds of discipline then are available, or susceptible, to these transgressive movements?

Elsewhere I have argued that relevant disciplines must at some level be homologues of one another, a relationship that guarantees the necessary disciplinary proximity.[74] The maintenance of "gaps" between disciplines or clusters of disciplines, of the kind lamented by Campbell, is in this account, essential for the particularity of scandalous space, practice throughout which is both within and without the relevant disciplines. Mark Cousins has referred to the particular permeability of architecture to the practices of others as constituting a "weak discipline."[75] I would argue that there is a spectrum of permeabilities but that permeability does not in itself, or necessarily, constitute a homological proximity.

The space, then, between homologically related disciplines is a space of potential scandal, and the act of transgression towards another discipline with which it shares homological traits, breaks free from disciplinary centres and triggers that scandal. Coles and Defert writing about interdisciplinary practice in general, emphasise this potentiality as a type of ambiguity, "it is only by maintaining the degree of uncertainty that interdisciplinary work bears – while simultaneously producing critiques of earlier sites of interdisciplinary practice – that new sites can be progressively opened up."[76]

So I propose that between the disciplines of propositional making – between architecture and archaeology in this case – lies a potential, interdisciplinary and scandalous space of production sketched out by Barbara Stafford in *Visual Analogy* as an "analogical universe,"[77] and triggered by particular transgressive practices. This book attempts to unravel, account for and then use that analogical universe through the transgressive, transdisciplinary, practice of architecture towards archaeology.

So what is it in archaeology that allows this type of productive interdisciplinary incursion from architecture? Archaeologist Michael Shanks has been speculating about the relationship of archaeology to design and craft since the early 1990s and his work provides one way of responding to this question. Shanks writes of his own discipline;

> *We also intend to sketch an archaeology which is not a passive reflection or representation of the things it unearths, but actively reconstructs the past, that is, constructs pasts anew. In this we stress that archaeology is a constructive project, a part of the present as well as of the past."*[78]

This view of the "project" of archaeology made through the simple expedient of removing the "re" to give "construction" shifts emphasis from the past in to the present. Indeed, in Shanks's view archaeology is not at all past-centred. For him, past-centred archaeology occludes its proper task; the production of the past in the present. Shanks argues, "to reproduce the past 'as it was,' to relive the past as a reflection, is to produce an image which hides the observing present."[79]

Shanks further situates archaeology as a productive, and not simply reproductive practice, explaining that, "archaeologists are in the business of designing contemporary culture."[80] Here he casts archaeology as a significant player in the making of the present, a form of social and cultural production not divorced from the physical act of its making and writes, "the experience of archaeology is not irrelevant and it is essential to consider those who experience the production of the past. Archaeology is not a neutral instrument for exploring the past but its theatre."[81] In this productive, physical theatre, the players may use a series of props, "archaeologists take what's materially left of the past and work on it intellectually and physically to produce knowledge through reports, papers, books, museum displays, TV programs, whatever."[82] Shanks is clear that it is the accumulation and assembly of these fragmentary artefacts which enables the archaeologist to construct a propositional narrative enacted in the present, or as Henrietta Moore explains, "this determination of origins by ends necessarily means that the past is constructed or reconstructed in terms of the present. Our creative representations of the past are shaped not by what we know to be true of the past, but by what we believe to be true of the present,"[83] as apposite a description of architecture as it is of archaeology. Shanks further acknowledges the reflexive influence that those props have exerted on the early practice of archaeology and writes of, "the place of scientific instruments in the work of the antiquarian, such as spade and quill, compass and rule. How did such instruments bring about the standardization of antiquarian research?"[84] This involuted interplay of past and present, through its instruments and media is enacted through the "theatre" of archaeology. Mike Pearson and Shanks write;

> *For me, it begins with a technical drawing [...]*
> *It is of the Black Gate, part of the new castle of Newcastle upon Tyne, in the north of England, 'newly' built from 1280. I had completed in 1980 a new survey of the well-preserved remains of this many-times altered building [...]. I was accurate, no more than a centimetre lost over fifty metres. Or so I thought, until I realised that the drafting paper I was using was highly susceptible to stretch and shrink in the damp January weather and by my gas fire in the garage, used as office, under the railway arches.*[85]

This fetishisation of the media and techniques of one's own discipline – the "props" which make its performance possible – will be familiar to those who work closely with and rely upon such objects, and these objects in particular (drafting paper and its behaviour) will be familiar not only to archaeologists like Shanks, but to many architects as well. The skills described in Shanks's situated tale of paper and moisture are craft skills and describe a craft mentality. For Richard Sennett that is simply, "the skill of making things well,"[86] Shanks's "stretch and shrink" aligning with my own memories of adjusting the draughting-taped corners of tracing paper – physically pushing the paper with my arms to re-stretch it after it had sagged a little overnight – fitting well with Sennett's assertion that, "all skills, even the most abstract, begin as bodily practices."[87] These are immediate acts of making; "intimate connection[s] between hand an head."[88]

At times, for Shanks – and others[89] – archaeology is a craft-based discipline. At other times this elides with his reading of design practice. He argues, for example, that the, "work of archaeology can and should be modeled as craft and design."[90] I would want to more definitively differentiate between craft and design; not to drive a wedge between them but to provide an account of their relationship to one another. Sennett suggests that craftsmanship may be summed up as, "the intimate relations between problem solving and problem finding, technique and expression, play and work,"[91] And for craft, the view of Jonathan Bean and Daniela Rosner seems more persuasive to me;

> *Perhaps craft is best thought of as a verb that represents the material translation of the work of design. As such, we may question the call for design to transform itself into some sort of supra-discipline intended to coordinate, corral, and control the work and craft of others* [92]

For them design-based disciplines should, "include

the mastery of a craft in the execution of design."[93]

Craft can be speculative, of course, but I would argue that this is a very limited form of immediate, inquisitive engagement with material; Sennett's, "problem solving and problem finding." In any case the corollary of this, the role that Shanks proposes for craft in archaeology, is rightly beyond the capabilities of design practice alone. Shanks and Randall H. McGuire write, "we suggest that the notion of craft that developed in the Arts and Crafts movement mends those rips in modern archaeology: reason from execution, theory from practice."[94] A worthy role indeed for craftsmanship, unavailable to design.

Design has an altogether different role in archaeological practice and clues to this nascent, hidden, speculative mode of production are present in Shanks's archaeological practice. Shanks and Christopher Tilley explain that, "for the subjective idealism of scientistic archaeology we substitute a view of the discipline as an hermeneutically informed dialectical science of past and present unremittingly embracing and attempting to understand the polyvalent qualities of the socially constructed world of the past and the world in which we live."[95] What then is it about design which means that it can be meaningfully said that some archaeological practices are forms of it? Or, put another way, why is design, just like reconstruction as practiced by archaeologists, a form of propositional making?

In architecture, as this book argues, "the tolerance of multiple solutions" offered by a design sensibility "seems to contrast greatly with other disciplines."[96] In particular this state of "tolerance" has not been the case within archaeology, at least not until the postprocessualist turn;[97] in the work of Ian Hodder and many others at Çatalhöyük, for example, a major archaeological project which overtly employs reflexive processes and encourages multiple interpretations. Archaeology is not part of Bryan Lawson's hierarchy of core design disciplines – those whose design practices are defined by their "tolerance" – however, his list of those which are is predictable;

> *Many forms of design then, deal with both precise and vague ideas, call for systematic and chaotic thinking, need both imaginative thought and mechanical calculation. However, a group of design fields seem to lie near the middle of the spectrum of design activity. The three-dimensional and environmental design fields of architecture, interior design, product and industrial design, urban and landscape design, all require the designer to produce beautiful and also practically useful and well-functioning end products.*[98]

But over twenty years earlier Donald Schön had already identified a shifting of these comfortable disciplinary "centres" warning that, "architecture, once the mother profession, now occupies a somewhat ambiguous position within the larger family."[99] The shift in thinking about design, from emphasising positivistic processes as Christopher Alexander and Herbert Simon did[100] to the reflexive circularity exemplified in the work of Schön and Ranulph Glanville,[101] is mirrored in archaeology in the shift from the scientific foundations of processual archaeologies of Lewis Binford, Philip Phillips and Colin Renfrew in 1950s, 1960s and 1970s to the reflexive, postprocessualisms of Hodder, Daniel Miller and Tilley. Shanks in particular describes archaeological processes thus;

> *a key archaeological concept of assemblage in connecting the understanding of design with a methodology that traces connections through fields of relations, as well as scrutinizes the features and qualities of an artifact.*[102]

He manages to identify what is similar in archaeology to other design disciplines although it is not clear that he thinks of archaeology as being one – only that design thinking is or would be useful, even essential, for it – and what is different and so unique to it;

> *design always attends to the past, has to, whether this is expressed in styling or not. The simple reason is that every design act has to take account of the current environment that determines design choices – the constraints of viability, feasibility, people's expectations. This environment is, of course, an inherited one, the result of decisions and processes that may reach back thousands of years (as do urban infrastructures).*[103]

Curiously missing from many discussions about design methodology is any analysis of how design is actually made – an analysis reserved for a different literature altogether, "nobody mentions drawing, the one common action of designers of all kinds"[104] as Jones felt compelled to exclaim. Cross states the centrality to design of drawing very simply, if quite normatively;

> *The designer's aim, therefore, is the communication of a specific design proposal. Usually, this is in the form of a drawing or drawings, giving both an overview of the artefact and particular details. Even the most imaginative design proposals must usually be communicated in rather prosaic working drawings, lists of parts, and so on.*[105]

> *Drawings [...] feature heavily in [the] generative phase of the design process, although at the earliest stages they will be just the designer's 'thinking with a pencil' and perhaps comprehensible only to him or her.*[106]

Both Schön and Glanville emphasise the extensive nature of drawing – that drawing is not simply the use of drawing instruments to make drawing products, but an extension of the designer themselves. Schön talks of "having a conversation" with a drawing, whilst Glanville characterises "design as a conversation, usually held via a medium such a paper and pencil, with an other (either an 'actual' other or oneself acting as an other) as the conversational partner. The word 'conversation' is used in a recognizable and everyday manner."[107] But drawing also has a social instrumentality underplayed in Cross's analysis;

drawing is used to order and structure the social interactions and social relations of the many actors who participate in a design project. It sets social hierarchies, defines a social agenda, and provides an important instrument through which the social production of architecture is organized.[108]

Indeed it is a central argument of this book that the instrumentalities of design and reconstruction are propositional in character – Dorst and Dijkhuis again;

Describing design as a process of reflection-in-action works particularly well in the conceptual stage of the design process, where the designer has no standard strategies to follow and is proposing and trying out problem/solution structures.[109]

This "proposing and trying out" (though not, as I have argued, the "problem/solution structures" more characteristic of craft) – the propositional character of design – is central to the disciplines which use it and characterises the practices employed by it. Crucially, this kind of proposition is underpinned by an abductive logical process. That is a process analogical in character described by Pragmatist philosopher Charles Sanders Peirce "who distinguished it from the other more well-known modes of inductive and deductive reasoning. [...] It is [...] the logic of conjecture [...] Design ability is therefore founded on the resolution of ill-defined problems by adopting a solution-focussing strategy and productive or appositional styles of thinking."[110]

If both design and reconstruction are forms of

propositional making then both gather together and do work upon fragmentary material. The difference in terminology signifies simply the type of fragment employed and the purported intention of any particular practitioner; the architect purports to practice in a future-facing mode – they design artefacts to be made in the future, whereas the archaeologist purports to practice in a past-facing mode – they reconstruct artefacts that were made in the past. In fact both the architect and the archaeologist practice acts of propositional making performed in the present through the indexical relationship between designer and artefact. Architectural critic Marco Frascari takes this performative reading of architecture and its ambiguous relationship to time and re-imagines it as a shamanistic process;[111] a reading of signs to establish the most propitious moment for its enactment through building construction. Here building is not the inevitable product of a design process, instead the design process searches for and makes available the moment when construction may begin, "using these analogous instruments, the opportunity for a project is developed. This is not simply a spatial procedure, but a mantic operation requiring careful timing and specific opportunities."[112] The "mantic" or divinatory process of design is seen as a ritualised use of "analogous instruments" such as drawings. These drawings-as-instruments for Frascari seem to probe time and space searching for an opportunity to manifest themselves as buildings;

> *An architectural projection is graphically divined through rules when the opportunity for construction arises. The translation of edifices into drawings and of drawing into edifices is the foundation of the mantic paradigm in architecture.*[113]

The architect's secret knowledge manifested through drawing and in drawings enables them to see the invisible (draw a plan by observing only the outside of a building), see backwards in time (draw a ruined building as if it were complete) and to see the future (design a building);

> *In this spirit, an architect can imagine, or more properly divine, a plan and section simply by observing an existing building. He can also reconstruct them from a ruined building and ultimately envision those of a building that doesn't yet exist. The common denominator of these operations is the capacity of the architect to formulate a graphic evocation of the invisible.*[114]

Yet I would argue that the architect is not the only holder of this secret knowledge, that in fact this knowledge is not secret, not quite; it is only hidden from some practitioners and consumers of it. In this account the archaeologist is also a designer and the full "divinatory" power of drawing and drawings is also available to them.

The simple observation that the practices of design-centred disciplines are available outside of those core disciplines no matter how policed they may seem to be begins to build an armature for a specifically archaeology-driven manifestation of design. For some, this site of speculative production in archaeology reveals itself in the performative act of excavation, Shanks and Mike Pearson's "archaeological excavation as performance event,"[115] as much as in the practice of drawing. Excavation and reconstruction are particular to archaeology and may also be cast as specifically creative, design-centred activities. McFadyen writes, "after all, excavation in archaeology is itself a practice and should therefore resonate directly with an architecture that exists in the making. What would a creative practice in archaeology be like, that does justice to architecture as process?"[116]

It seems then that archaeology is already a creative discipline in its own right, employing design-based drawing practices. Conversely in architecture drawing is either, conventionally, an intermediate stage to building construction or, at times, the principal work of the architect. Seen through the lens of archaeology, however, opportunities are provided for different and productive methodologies and for more inclusive disciplinary goals, for example: the "constructive practices"[117] of medieval building identified by Alberto Pérez-Gómez and Louise Pelletier which to some extent still have their analogue in archaeological practices (see Site of Encounter: Must Farm); in Robin Evans's lament that "architectural space would remain, one way or another, limited by and bonded to the pictures that normally gave access to it,"[118] though this need not be the case if architecture were to look outside of itself for other kinds of "pictures," or in Jonathan Hill's critique of the strong, professionalised, "conservative and self-protective,"[119] centre of architectural practice and his promotion of "architecture by accident"[120] which in this account is the "accident" of interdisciplinarity.

In archaeology, the drawn recording of objects and their contexts has also been seen as idealistically scientific; that is, of the New Archaeology[121] or, later, peripheral to the consequent acts of interpretation, as the postprocessualists would have it. But the drawn artefacts of both of these disciplines compared are more than simply evidence of historical coincidence but of deeper homological resemblances and the more profound analogical motivations identified and prefaced above and further developed below.

The Undisciplinary

Architects do not make buildings; they make drawings of buildings.[122]

Nowadays, we know what kinds of drawings architects make. They have been codified by tradition, by profession and by legislation.[123]

Having worked in architectural practice since 1993 and having begun my architectural studies in 1986 I am in no doubt that over the last thirty years many of the tools and techniques most closely associated with the practice of architecture have been abandoned and superseded by new tools, techniques and associated practices. Some of these tools and techniques had remained unchanged for centuries; Maya Hambly comprehensively describes the shifts in drawing instrument design and function from the late Renaissance[124] until what Mario Carpo has described as "the digital turn."[125] "Not long ago, in the nineties," wrote Carpo in 2010, "no one doubted that a 'digital revolution' was in the making – in architecture as in all aspects of life, science, and art."[126] Yet Carpo is describing a revolution which, in his view, never happened – at least not in the way we think it did. "Today" he continues, "the very expression 'digital revolution' has fallen into disuse, if not into disrepute."[127] His view, echoing that of Peter Eisenman writing in 1992, is that the object of architecture has remained relatively stable. Eisenman wrote, "since architecture has traditionally housed value as well as fact, one would imagine that architecture would have been greatly transformed. But this is not the case."[128] In fact I would argue for a greater change than either Carpo writing relatively recently, or Eisenman writing nearly thirty years ago, admit to. In any case, in this account the absolute degree of disciplinary change is less relevant than how the tools and techniques of that discipline, whether analogue or digital, mirror and influence that change and what happens when those tools and techniques are no longer needed or are considered irrelevant to that discipline. In addition to these abandonments is another, related, class of tools and techniques; those which have only ever been seen as peripheral to more mainstream architectural drawing, rarely used in conventional architectural practice[129] and so remain unadopted by it or any other discipline. In both cases – the abandoned and the unadopted – I propose that their loose connection to normative disciplinary centres enables them to be more readily used in the scandalous space between disciplines. These tools and techniques are, or have become, I argue, *undisciplined*.[130] They are neither disciplined by centralised professions, nor do they seek to discipline those interdisciplinary practitioners who use them. The category of the undisciplined as used here has been developed through what I have called a Chronotopic Chart. Introduced below in Chapter 2 the Chart is a device useful for establishing non-temporally adjacent connections between, in this case, architectural and archaeological tools, techniques, key figures and events.

The impact that the tools and techniques of architecture have had on the buildings they have helped build has depended upon their accuracy, their legibility, their portability, their relative transparency as a medium, as well as upon their reproducibility. These attributes and contexts; the tools that made them, the media of which they were, and continue to be made, and the practices within which those tools and that media are embedded is, in Pierre Bourdieu's terms, the habitus of the practitioners of design-centred and to some extent design-engaged disciplines. Bourdieu has variously defined the habitus as systems of "durable, transposable dispositions,"[131] a "mental and corporeal schemata of perceptions, appreciations, and action,"[132] and as a "generative principle of regulated improvisations."[133] The habitus becomes, in this account, embodied in objects and their spatial relationships. It is also, crucially, "the product of internalization of the principles of a cultural arbitrary capable of perpetuating itself after PA [pedagogic action] has ceased."[134] For the architect this includes the tendency for arbitrarily selected drawing projection types – say orthographic as opposed to perspectival systems – to seem to become natural and inevitable products of the practice of architecture itself. An "internalization" perpetuated through the training regimes of schools of architecture and commercial practice. This is truer still in departments of archaeology where students are trained to make drawings in even more tightly prescribed modes than in architecture, perhaps because archaeology courses tend to be shorter than architectural ones, or that archaeological drawing is rarely seen as central to archaeological practice. In the U.K., for example, illustration is taught, if at all, as a single module at undergraduate level and planning is picked up on the job or at training excavations. In the U.S.A., by contrast, the formal teaching of drawing is rare and in any case there are no universal standards to teach.[135]

What would happen to these drawing practices were they freed, a little, from such "internalization"? The disciplinary shifts described above leave casualties; abandoned or unadopted drawing types in particular. These undisciplined drawing types enable the practitioners of them to make work freer of Bourdieu's "internalization" than would otherwise be possible. They are drawing types which, I would argue, are useful but which are also external to any centralising professionalised discipline. As Andrew Barry and Georgina Born comment, "a commitment to a discipline is a way of ensuring that certain disciplinary methods and concepts are used rigorously and that undisciplined and undisciplinary objects, methods and concepts are ruled out."[136] But what happens if, instead, we ruled them in? The Chronotopic Chart outlines a number of such undisciplinary drawing tools and techniques, and highlighting just three will give a flavour of their general character:

(1) *The Multi-Informational Image*; a type of

drawing made briefly prominent by Giovanni Battista Piranesi in the mid-eighteenth-century to become almost immediately abandoned after his death; the term 'multi-informational' was coined by archaeologist Susan Dixon;[137] (2) *The Mise-en-Scène Illustration*; used ubiquitously in archaeology but incorporated almost unrecognisably into architecture through the "staffage"[138] of presentation drawings. This drawing type has been too universally useful to have ever been adopted by any particular discipline; (3) *The Exploded Drawing*; a type used infrequently in architecture but which is employed ubiquitously in many vernacular drawing practices and incorporated, I would argue (though again almost unrecognisably) into archaeology through the Harris Matrix and other types of seriation diagram. Again this drawing type has remained unadopted by any particular discipline.

Detailed analysis of undisciplined drawing types is beyond the scope of this book but I have written about them elsewhere.[139]

Archaeology is Like Architecture in Reverse

Presented on the one hand with a section drawn by an archaeologist and, on the other, with one drawn by an architect, what is to be made of their visual similarities? Fig. 4 shows a contemporary section through the typical generic foundations of a load-bearing masonry wall. It is a technical drawing I made for a client's basement extension, and is propositional in its intent. Figure 5 reproduces a section through the foundations of an existing structure. It is also a technical drawing though, in this instance, intended for archaeologists.[140]

Are the resemblances between these drawings to be found in their graphic likeness and in their similarity of subject matter alone? How are their differences to be interpreted? In particular, what is to be made of drawings (for example, Fig. 6 is another survey and reconstruction this time by a nineteenth-century Prix de Rome winner)[141] produced by those whose discipline at the time of their drawing's production described itself as neither architecture nor archaeology and whose drawings are difficult to categorise along current, normative, disciplinary lines? Homologies in the development of architecture and archaeology are evident in the visual resemblance between their drawings, of which Figures 4, 5 and 6 are but three examples which, despite divergences, illustrate continued commonalities between the tools and techniques of the two disciplines.

The Darwinian concept of divergence[142] can help explain these shared visual similarities. We know that the common ancestry of archaeology and architecture, embodied in the drawings reproduced below (and countless others like them) is complex.

For example, it is clear that architecture is an older discipline than archaeology; their relationship to antiquarianism, their most recent common ancestor, though a direct one, is not straightforward to parse. Also difficult to unravel is the extent to which these disciplines have since diverged, each developing within its own "isolated environment"[143] and then becoming professionalised in order to shore itself against intrusions from cognate disciplines. There would also seem to be hidden resemblances between architecture and archaeology which are not straightforwardly manifested in their drawing practices; terms, tools and techniques which may not look or function in an obviously similar way – whose resemblance have become occluded. In this account, for a homological resemblance to prevail, the tools or techniques in question must simply have been the same thing at the point in the past at which they began to diverge from each other in either form or function or both. What is pertinent here is that despite the persistent similarities between the purposes to which these drawings and others have been put, the purported objects of each of their respective disciplines have, since mid-nineteenth-century disciplinary professionalisation, become radically estranged.

But the overt differences are important too because they conceal yet deeper resemblances; for example

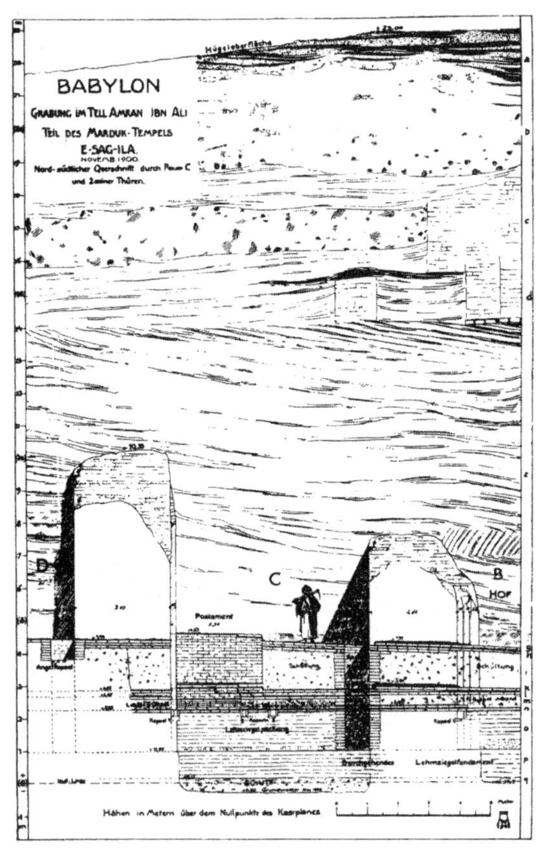

Fig. 4 Foundation and Basement Retaining Wall, Hammersmith Grove, Zambelli, A., Bates Zambelli Architects, 2006.
Robert Koldewey, Excavation in Tell Amran ibn Ali. Part of the Marduk Temple, 1900. From Koldewey, Robert. Das Wieder Erstehende Babylon. Die Bisherigen Ergebnisse Der Deutschen Ausgrabungen ... Mit 255 Abbildungen Und Planen, Davon 7 in Farbigem Lichtdruck. pp. vii. 328. 1913.

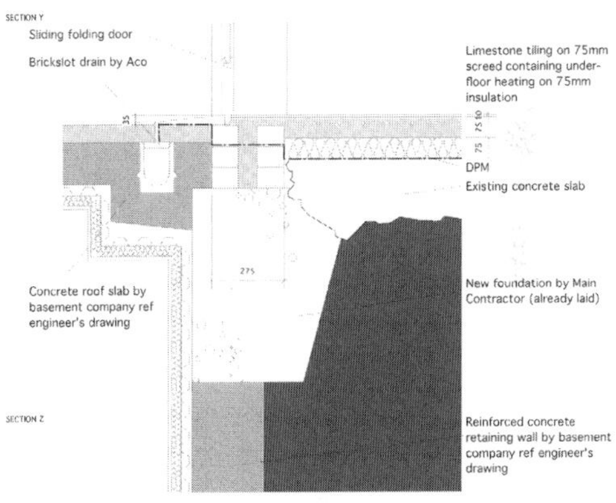

Figs. 5 and 6 Jean-François-Julien Ménager, The Temple of Antoninus Pius and Faustina. 1809. From: Cassanelli, Roberto, and Massimiliano David. 2002. Ruins of Ancient Rome: the drawings of French architects who won the Prix de Rome, 1786-1924 (J.P. Getty Museum: Los Angeles). 81.

to return to my, and Ménager's drawings, the conventions of delineating the edges of a structure (in architecture) or feature (in archaeology) – the variation in terminology is instructive – are sufficiently different to be able to identify and posit reasons for those differences. Whereas the architect must, in general, propose a structure in defiance of its immediate context; the foundation must resist the ground within which it sits, the archaeologist instead proposes a feature which, often, is as important (though this will depend upon the intended audience of the drawing) as the context of the matrix within which it sits. In short, often the architect's drawing emphasises strong edges whilst that of the archaeologist is often softer, highlighting subtle changes in the, "compaction," "composition" or "particle size" of the surrounding terrain.[144] The Ménager drawing, and many like it from the Prix de Rome 'envois,' tend to accentuate surface; even when the drawings are sections or sectional elevations. Often the sectioned material is rendered white or pale with little detail so as not to distract from the verisimilitude of the reconstructed elevational surface. Their sameness, though, is as deep as these differences. In fact, resemblance and difference are part of the same analogical system of interdisciplinary signification.

It would take an exhaustive survey of drawings from both architecture and archaeology, made for a wide diversity of purposes and by a multitude of different hands, to make definitive assertions about general practices and their associated products, and that is beyond the scope of this book. Yet the few examples above show, I would argue, a clear differentiation between drawing conventions and, simultaneously, a sometimes occluded resemblance, a resemblance which resides in the fact that, and as this book argues, archaeologists have always, just as have architects, made propositional drawings. Two brief quotations will suffice to demonstrate something of the depth and character of this resemblance, as archaeologist Simon James explains recounting his own experience of excavation and recording;

> *As we dug I created interpretive sketches of the buildings, based on the groundplans, the form of the foundations, and the properties of the timber [...] and other materials known or expected to have been used.*[145]

James is describing a design process; as he draws, he speculates about what the remains he describes might be reconstructed into – his "interpretive sketches" are, it seems to me, propositional. To quote Alain Schnapp on Jorge Luis Borges, "isn't the archaeologist often taken for a discoverer? The discoverer must not compel the reality of the past but imagine it."[146] Working from this 'imaginative' – that is speculative – and propositional basis, I hope to establish the mechanisms of resemblance at work between architecture and archaeology and which operate despite their divergence and the subsequent isolationism briefly outlined above, and which, I would argue, set pre-conditions for the interdisciplinary, visual, analogical practices required for navigation through scandalous space.

If, as this book argues, the potency of interdisciplinary work between architecture and archaeology relies upon their shared homological resemblance – their historically interconnected development – then understanding the mechanisms of this homological resemblance becomes central to its meaningful manipulation. Recall that in Scandalous Space an homology is a relationship of common or closely connected origin between disciplines; a relationship which enables meaningful interdisciplinary work to occur in the space between otherwise strong disciplinary centres.

As Bourdieu describes it in a social practice context, "a relation of homology [is one] of diversity within homogeneity"[147] essential structures remain unchanged but still allow for enormous variety; a variety which may, somewhat ironically, conceal that variety.

> *The wing of a bird is homologous to the wing of a bat as a derivative of the forelimb. The common ancestors of birds and bats possessed forelimbs of a similar basic construction, from which the wings are derived in both cases. The wing of a bird, however, is not homologous to the wing of a bat as a wing, since the forelimbs of the common amniote ancestors of birds and bats did not have the form of wings.*[148]

For an archaeologist or architect designing or reconstructing non or not yet existing buildings, where is the "third thing" to which any two terms in a homological relationship must relate?

In some ways the relationships of architecture and archaeology to antiquarianism are well understood – but I would want to emphasise antiquarianism as that last common ancestor of modern, professional architecture and archaeology, contextualising antiquarian pursuits within their networks of instruments and media. This relationship is crucial to what follows because it explains why it is possible to work meaningfully between the, now, definitively separate, professionalised, disciplines of architecture and archaeology.

Drawing and Time

> *above all, all excavation is fabrication. The object or monument is only brought to light through the act of seeking it, and whilst observing a certain number of rules of study and interpretation isn't the archaeologist often taken for a discoverer? The discoverer must not compel the reality of the past but imagine it.*[149]

I have been arguing that the design practices of architecture and the reconstructive practices of archaeology are, in important respects, both kinds of propositional practice and examining the interdisciplinary framework, through antiquarianism, which reveals this all but occluded unity of practice. For, once broken, the ancient discipline of architecture-antiquarianism cannot simply be stitched back together; Mary Shelley's "gloomy monster" invoked by Stafford[150] is not interdisciplinary – it is less, not more, than the sum of its parts – the sundered disciplines must, can only, be used together, simultaneously. Through analyses of the existing tools and techniques of each discipline – including what, in *Instrumental Reconstruction* below, I term 'conceptual disciplinary tools' – I examine how the recently divided practices of these design-disciplines-made-professions may benefit from re-combinations of the systematic scientific (but not only scientific) methodologies of archaeology and the speculative inventiveness of architecture.

Those practitioners whose discipline is normally, or is often, drawing-centred; animators, artists, architects, engineers, cartographers, product designers, graphic designers, illustrators, or those practitioners whose discipline – or their particular practice of it – is not drawing-centred but who regularly engage with drawing in some way (such disciplines are referred to as drawing-engaged in this book); anthropologists, archaeologists, geographers, scientists; their disciplines are in part defined by the products of those drawing practices and in some cases by the tools used to make those products. Robin Evans in particular notices this tendency;

> *A plan, which can be any shape, may tend to be rectangular for a host of reasons, but the internal logic of parallel projection will push it that way too. Five minutes at a drawing board will convince anyone unfamiliar with the technique that this is the way things have to be set out. The instruments at your disposal will lead you to produce frontal pictures of the several sides of boxes as soon as you have gained the slightest idea of what you are doing.*[151]

Or as anthropologist Clifford Geertz argues in a more generalised way;

> *the shapes of knowledge are always ineluctably local, indivisible from their instruments and their encasements. One may veil this fact with ecumenical rhetoric, or blur it with strenuous theory, but one cannot really make it go away.*[152]

I have been arguing that the representational drawing practices of architecture are embodied in those practices and instruments and also, because of its latent design practices and the historical coincidences it shares with architecture, in archaeology too. In this account, this pair of linked professions are further understood first as disciplined practices nurtured and developed within the constraints of their parent professions, and secondly, through the examination of particular drawing techniques – techniques either overlooked by the disciplines or abandoned by them – which enable a loosening of their respective disciplinary constraints. To loosen those disciplinary constraints first requires an understanding of how those constraints have come to be established, and how they operate.

Although I have been explicitly examining drawing practices in architecture and archaeology, it would be impossible to address these disciplines, and archaeology in particular, without touching upon one other. American archaeologist Philip Phillips notoriously wrote in 1955 that, "New World archaeology is anthropology or it is nothing."[153] Although this observation related to the particularly dependent relationship, as Phillips and others saw it, of archaeology to anthropology and to history, the general feeling that, "the archaeologist must borrow his theoretical underpinning from the field of study his work happens to serve"[154] was, according to Colin Renfrew, widespread at the time.[155] This "Great Divide"[156] between archaeology and anthropology as Renfrew described it in 1980, stemmed from an assumption, he writes, by the early pioneers of institutionalised American archaeology, that the paucity of physical remains in North America required that an anthropological narrative must be the only narrative worth telling.

This ambiguous relationship continues to this day and generates a steady stream of literature and associated hand-wringing. A 2003 book referring also to the Phillips quotation observed that, "this uncertainty has not abated, and nearly 50 years later the relationship [between anthropology and archaeology] has become more strained."[157] Others are more relaxed about the connections between the two, "anthropological thought is infused into all strands of archaeology" wrote Chris Gosden in 1999.[158] Less flexibly, and perhaps ironically, the current website of the Society for American Archaeology explains that, "archaeology is the study of the ancient and recent human past through material remains. It is a subfield of anthropology, the study of all human culture."[159]

By contrast the hegemony of the 'splitters' in the U.K. can be seen in the work of contemporary archaeologists and anthropologists concerned with the teasing out, forging or re-establishing of relationships between archaeology, architecture, art and anthropology, the absolute separation of which for them is seen as problematic. Tim Ingold, for example, through his, *The 4 A's: Anthropology, Archaeology, Art and Architecture* seminars[160] at the University of Aberdeen, analysed how art and anthropology may share goals and methodologies, and likewise for architecture and archaeology; how they may share homologous aims. Ingold wrote in 2011, concerning the making of his associated book *Redrawing Anthropology*, that its production was;

> *driven by an ambition to restore anthropology to life, and by the conviction that drawing – understood in the widest sense as a linear movement that leaves an impression or trace of one kind or another – must be central to our attempts to do so.*[161]

And it is this, "impression or trace," which fleshes out the move, in this book, towards a drawing, and drawing instrument-driven disciplinary account. The particularity of the relationship between architecture and anthropology, though not central to the argument here, serves to shed some light upon parallel interdisciplinarities in architecture and archaeology.

The making, strengthening, erasing and re-making of normative disciplinary centres, of which the briefest of accounts above of the fluxes in the landscape of twentieth-century American anthropological/archaeological disciplinarity is but one, is not unusual. Equivalent accounts for architecture, antiquarianism and archaeology in Europe may be told, though, are beyond the scope of this book, but all demonstrate that these shifts within and across disciplines which, either centrally or even only peripherally, use drawing practices are commonplace and on-going. I would also ask what forces drive the formation of these centres; reinforcing some disciplines, proscribing others and ascribing value to them within the matrix of those other disciplines and professions. These relationships work to reinforce each other – they establish the habitus; Pierre Bourdieu's, "generative principle of regulated improvisations,"[162] and so define the discipline *per se*. In this view disciplinary centres are strengthened through self-replication; the establishment of learned institutions, university departments and, in architecture, the protection of either title or function through statute. But it is also a central contention of this book that the close resemblance of many practices, tools and techniques of archaeology and architecture, facilitate movement across those disciplines and work between them. That, in particular, it is the relationship between the drawn line and the drawing practice (either drawing-centred or drawing-engaged) within which it situates itself, and its functions – either propositional or descriptive – which provide the immediate evidence of this resemblance.

Scandalous Practice

Throughout this book I characterise interdisciplinary, analogy-sensitive, space as 'scandalous.' The term scandal derives from Claude Lévi-Strauss's *The Elementary Structures of Kinship* which, recast in this account, provides a medium for the kind of interdisciplinary practice outlined above.[163] Lévi-Strauss divides social praxis into that which is "natural" and which spontaneously obeys universal laws, and the "cultural" which tends towards imposed norms and which allows itself to be contingently rule-governed. Lévi-Strauss asks us to, "suppose then that everything universal in man relates to the natural order, and is characterized by spontaneity, and that everything subject to a norm is cultural and is both relative and particular."[164] But for Lévi-Strauss there are also situations where both of these erstwhile mutually exclusive categories are able to operate simultaneously, for example, in the taboo against incest. Lévi-Strauss writes, "here therefore is a phenomenon which has the distinctive characteristics both of nature and of its theoretical contradiction, culture. The prohibition of incest has the universality of bent and instinct, and the coercive character of law and institution."[165] Lévi-Strauss provides a lengthy account of his evidence for the universality of the incest taboo explaining the occasional occurrence of consanguineous marriage, amongst other exceptions, as differences in degree rather than fact. The result, for him, of this unresolved conflict is a "scandal;"

> *We are then confronted with a fact, or rather, a group of facts, which [...] are not far removed from a scandal: we refer to that complex group of beliefs, customs, conditions and institutions described succinctly as the prohibition of incest, which presents, without the slightest ambiguity, and inseparably combines, the two characteristics in which we recognize the conflicting features of two mutually exclusive orders.*[166]

Put another way, where a particular social activity conforms to both spheres simultaneously, that is, where it ordinarily belongs within one realm of activity but allows itself to be governed by the contingent rules of another, Lévi-Strauss says that a scandal occurs. Of course Lévi-Strauss's exemplar is one of strong social taboo whereas interdisciplinary practice is, generally, somewhat less proscribed.

Rather than his unresolved confrontation between the "natural" and the "cultural" of the incest taboo, instead I propose, in this book, a confrontation between that category of making activities which are not rule-governed for any given practitioner, set against the normal making activities for that same practitioner which are rule-governed.

What happens, for example, when expert practitioners who would normally practice within their own discipline and within the extraordinary legal constraints which govern that discipline – for example engineers making cars or bridges, or architects designing buildings – begin to practice outside of their ordinary area of expertise, but in a way which renders them more liable than non-experts for the outcomes of their work? Those practitioners begin to operate at the fringes of the law; the engineer building a go-cart, perhaps, the architect erecting a shed. This kind of making is normal, of course; both activities appear to be natural or universal practices – building toys for children[167] or small vernacular buildings[168] – anyone might have a go. These activities only become problematic when things go wrong; the shed collapses onto a visitor or the go-cart fails at speed, ploughing into passers-by. For the professional, laws of caveat venditor[169] obtain and they are rendered extraordinarily liable for those incidents. In this account, the situation of the architect practising outside of their discipline and navigating towards a homologically related one, is not legally ambiguous – not quite, and certainly that is not the focus of this argument – instead it is ambiguous in terms of disciplinary affiliation; here, loosely following Lévi-Strauss, it is 'scandalous.'

Like Lévi-Strauss's taboo, the interdisciplinary scandal necessarily remains unresolved. These forms of practice are brought on by what Jacques Derrida describes as a "rupture" or a "redoubling"[170] and Lévi-Strauss's "scandal" as, "something [which] no longer tolerates the nature/culture opposition."[171] Propositional making in this scandalous space is the knowing but non-professional use of the tools and techniques of one discipline within the ordinary professional field of another related one and scandalous artefacts are the unresolved and hence fertile products of this kind of practice.

I argued earlier that movement across scandalous space requires navigation through tacking manoeuvres. These 'tacks' are analogical in character and scandalous space is logically structured and that it is this logical structure which ultimately makes Stafford's "analogical universe"[172] a legible, and not capricious, space for "sites of encounter." Working at the intersections of "neurobiology, cognitive science and the new philosophy of mind,"[173] Stafford has found common, interwoven, ground between those categories in visual culture. Although recently more concerned with neuroscientific connections with the visual arts, between 1991 and 2001 Stafford wrote a series of books and curated exhibitions centred upon the "history and theory of imaging and visualization modalities."[174] These works seek to contextualise contemporary, visually-centred, cultural practices and to re-legitimise, as she sees it, this re-emergence of pre-Enlightenment visual practice. A re-emergence, I argue, from logical and cognitive processes founded upon homological resemblance.

The homological lineages of, for example, birds and bats or, architecture and civil engineering, are relatively straightforward to trace. In the one case anatomical dissection and the fossil record provide sufficient evidence for the common ancestry of avian and mammalian anatomy. In the other, the disciplinary histories of two of the main modern professions which concern themselves with the construction of the designed environment is equally well documented.[175] The commonalities in the lineages of other disciplines are more complex to unpick. However, this book argues that it is this very commonality and its complexity which enables the transdisciplinary practitioner to navigate analogically between them.

What Georges Cuvier, the great early cataloguer and organiser of the natural world, begins by shifting emphasis, "from [a] description of the identifiable members of an organism, and classification by description,"[176] towards a more morphologically connected homological system of organisation, I trace forward to the work of anthropologist Alfred Gell. Gell writes at length in *Art and Agency* about abduction;[177] the motivating force which binds together the various agents in the network of relations which define, in Gell's analysis, art practice; indexes (artworks), artists (makers of artworks), recipients (audiences for artworks) and prototypes (that which is represented by the artwork). The ability of these agents to act abductively upon one another resides, I argue, in their pre-disposing homological relationship. So where Gell says, "I propose that the category of indexes relevant to our theory are those which permit the abduction of agency and specifically social agency,"[178] I propose instead that the category of architectural and archaeological practices relevant to this account are those which permit the "abduction of agency," a permission founded upon the homological proximity, through antiquarianism, of architecture and archaeology.

Analogy provides a method of practice for navigating and working directly in the space where homologically proximate disciplinary influences interact, and it is within this "space" that the resemblance between design and reconstruction is most clearly revealed. To make interdisciplinary work here amongst the complex, oblique, network of relationships established through homological proximity requires careful navigation employing analogical tacking movements. For Stafford, it is within this "synthesising" space that, "the central idea of the analogical world view"[179] exists, that;

> *all physical phenomena, from fallen stars, to Florentine stones, to magnified fleas, to the most skilfully chased silver goblets, can be cross-referenced, linked in reconciling explanation by the informed imagination.*[180]

As I have implied above, it is easier to see the formal similarities between, say, a toaster and a building, than it is to see the occluded resemblances between Stafford's; "fallen stars," "Florentine stones," "magnified fleas" and "chased silver goblets"[181] I say 'occluded' because the network of connections between the various artefacts has become too complex to adequately describe homologically. In this 'universe' only analogical connections provide the necessary looseness to make interdisciplinary work.

Frascari shares Stafford's view of the interconnectedness of the "analogical universe" and places Euclid alongside Plato and Aristotle as the triumvirate of founders of analogical thinking;

> *in Euclid's hands, the manipulation of geometric figures became the highest standard of logical reasoning. Yet these same manipulations were employed in divinatory procedures as a form of natural writing to be deciphered from the chance*

arrangement of things such as stars or lots or cracks.[182]

A more explicit connection between Peirce's philosophy and Stafford's visual analogy is made by Frascari in his 1986 paper *Semiotica Ab Edendo*, "in working out his semiotic doctrine Charles S. Peirce [...] deals with the inferential and iconic creation of images, an act which brings together realities which are more or less remote."[183]

The practices with which this book is concerned are made at the juxtaposition of the disciplines of architecture and archaeology in scandalous space where their, "realities [...] are more or less remote." In this scandalous space, between homologically related disciplines which resemble one another and of which architecture and archaeology are but two, a form of interdisciplinary, analogical practice is required. Inevitably one discipline will be dominant – the one in which the practitioner is expert – and the other is the target discipline – here the practitioner is an outsider. The base discipline is in an analogical relationship with the target practice and the practitioner, working there, we might term the *Analogist.*

Chapter 2

London Stone Reconstructed

Throughout this book, I have been investigating what happens when architectural practice is allowed to purposefully and directedly spill towards the discipline of archaeology, where archaeology is construed as a design discipline, a discipline of speculative, propositional making. As Figure 1 maps, and as the 'sites of encounter' describe, I have tested transdisciplinary techniques of resistance to stronger or weaker disciplinary centres. I do not argue for any particular centralising malice on the part of strong professionalised disciplines, since disciplinary centres do serve important cultural functions. Interesting, ground-breaking and moving work continues, of course, to be made deep within architecture and archaeology. For work to be self-critical it must look not just to its own centres, nor even to its peripheries (in fact I argue that there are no peripheries as such, merely a weakening of the influences of disciplines) instead we must look to the space between disciplines where centralising disciplinary influences are weak and available to interdisciplinary practice. This book argues for particular qualities of this scandalous space; I hinted above at the exstence a Peircean logico-cognitive network, below I will argue for a Deleuzian felt-like "smooth space"[184] but where both systems are conducive to strategies of analogical navigation.

London Stone

In a niche at low level behind a decorative grille facing the road at 111 Cannon Street, London, and built into its wall is London Stone its home since 1962 (Fig. 7).[185]

The Stone has proved to be something of an embarrassment to those disciplined professionals who might otherwise have claimed ownership over its cultural presence. It is difficult to account for archaeologically since techniques of cut and cover, employed in the building of the Inner Circle Line

Fig. 7 Eleanor Suess, The Moves of London Stone tour [still from pre-tour footage]. 2013, Digital film.

in 1884 directly underneath Cannon Street, would have swept away any and all of the Stone's ancient contexts. The only visual reconstructive work of the site – now largely under Cannon Street Railway Station – was done in the 1960s by archaeological illustrator Alan Sorrell.[186] At that time the remains were thought to be the palace of the Roman Governor of London. In his *Roman London*[187] Sorrell sketches-in an entrance to the 'Palace' complex, a closer look at which reveals it to be a generic Roman triumphal arch. Sorrell makes an educated guess as to the appearance of these entrance structures since very little of the earlier Roman buildings have been found and plotted, and nothing at all of its entrance sequence or, perhaps, as I shall go on to explain, only a very small piece of it; the fragment known as London Stone.

The area around Cannon Street Station was extensively bombed during the Second World War but in the decade before its redevelopment City of London archaeologist Peter Marsden was able to record various features that were still to be found.[188] One of Marsden's drawings shows a feature near, or at, the probable entrance to the complex and which he has labelled, "site of London Stone." These drawings remain the only serious attempt *archaeologically* to situate the Stone. But neither is the London Stone comfortably an architectural artefact even though, since the early nineteenth-century, architects and their developer and contractor-clients have attempted to incorporate it into the buildings which have hosted it. Indeed the Stone and its immediate enclosure are listed by English Heritage as Grade II*[189] a category usually reserved for historically significant buildings or recognisable fragments of buildings, rather than the Scheduled Ancient Monument designation, an alternative category intended for archaeological sites and objects.[190] Reflecting this confusion, plans for its incorporation into new buildings proposed for the site have been fraught. Most recently the redevelopment of 111 Cannon Street has seen the Stone temporarily re-housed in the Museum of London and, since 2018, returned to its ancient location (more or less) in a contemporary re-working of its previous housing. The status of the Stone for heritage professionals is even more puzzling; the verifiable history of London Stone is scanty and interwoven with mythologies both ancient and recently fabricated. Very few have been able to agree, for example, on the form or content of the textual information adjacent to the Stone. Should a new housing be designed for it? Perhaps it should be reconstructed to resemble one, or some, of its earlier recorded settings? Or perhaps nothing should be done – it is, after all, a rather unlovely lump of rock with little discernible evidence of its original form. Since I have argued that design and reconstruction are closely inter-related forms of propositional making – that they manifest, in common, essential drives and ambitions – a reconstruction of London Stone would, then, also be a design. In this view even to do nothing, when commentators and heritage professionals alike publicly and loudly decry the modest and uncared-for state of the Stone and its setting,[191] would also be propositional. This is not to argue that 'doing nothing' is a category of propositional making in its own right, rather that choosing not to design in the insistent face of the forces of regeneration and redevelopment, or not to reconstruct because that would close off a myriad of unchosen possibilities, are nevertheless options with the force of propositional consequence.

The rest of this chapter, therefore, is devoted to making alternative, speculative reconstructions of London Stone through the twinned practices of design and reconstruction. Navigating from architecture, as I necessarily must, I have chosen to call these speculative experiments 'reconstructions' to emphasise the disciplinary shift towards archaeology. These reconstructions make use, not just of architectural knowledge, tools, techniques and associated practices, but also the undisciplinary tools and techniques outlined above, to reveal and use the latent reconstructive practices of architecture and design practices of archaeology. They will be designs; speculative reconstructions of the artefact of which London Stone was, and will, be part. These categories of reconstruction have been developed out of my architecturally-centred response to the tools, techniques and practices of archaeology as I have become acquainted with them during the course of my transdisciplinary journey outwards from architecture. That research has sometimes been desk-based, sometimes more physical, and the range of reconstruction types discussed below reflects this. It is not an exhaustive list, instead it represents those forms of reconstruction which I found most readily 'offered,' in the sense Stafford uses for Latour's 'proposition,' "an invit[ation]" for architecture and archaeology "to relate in a new manner," where both "diverge from their customary paths to venture onto territory which, although it appears foreign from each of their unique vantage points, nonetheless belongs to an interdependent existence."[192] That is to say, the categories or types, and their contents, have changed over the course of researching this book and they will, no doubt, continue to change.

The reconstructions fall into a series of types which I have characterised in the annotated list below. Fuller summaries of each category will begin each section proper:

Chronotopic Reconstruction: The chronotope is used as a tool for making reconstructions;

specific resemblances across architectural and archaeological tools, techniques and events are identified regardless of their place in time or chronological sequence. Chronotopic reconstructions are mappings of these discrete instances made through Bakhtinian temporal "thickening" accompanied by spatial, "charging" "responsive" to that thickening – that is, time thickened with, "plot and history."[193]

Choreographic Reconstruction: London Stone is characterised by the relative stability of its siting with, however, periodic oscillations around that location. Detached from its point of origin it slowly roams Cannon Street. Retracing its steps, this form of reconstruction maps the presences, absences and movements of the artefact.

Instrumental Reconstruction: The nature of any reconstruction or design is dependent upon the tools used to make it. Instrumental Reconstruction is not so much a category in its own right as it is a description and a method pertinent to all other categories.

Chimaeric Reconstruction: A form of reconstruction where fragments of disparate and apparently unconnected provenance are juxtaposed analogically, the catalyst for their generation of meaning as a whole is provided by their context. Here, London Stone is reconstructed, through drawing, from those contexts themselves.

These reconstructions are propositional; like designs they draw on and gather together fragments, as we have seen in Shanks, Pearson and Tilley above, for their performance in the present. The conclusion in the next chapter contains a final reconstruction called (tautologically for emphasis) *A propositional reconstruction*.

Chronotopic Reconstruction

The drawing instruments of architecture, archaeology and antiquarianism, and the drawings made with them may be used as chronotopic devices to calibrate their divergence (in terms of practice) from each other, making possible an alternative narrative for the development of those disciplines. The idea of the chronotope was developed by Russian philosopher and literary critic Mikhail Bakhtin, and for literature he says that it;

> expresses the inseparability of space and time [...] spatial and temporal indicators are fused into one carefully thought-out, concrete whole. Time, as it were, thickens, takes on flesh, becomes artistically visible; likewise, space becomes charged and responsive to the movements of time, plot and history[194]

One way of explaining the disciplinary resemblances between architecture and archaeology is to understand something of their development across time. If it is true that architecture and archaeology share, broadly, not simply certain tools, techniques and associated practices, but also hidden and unstated general aims, occluded by the language of their respective disciplines, then it will be possible to look at the relationship between those disciplines chronotopically. That is, the early reconstructive practices of architects, and the origins of archaeology as a profession within the British antiquarian movement "thicken[ed]," as Bakhtin writes above, through their tool use and artefact production. These unstated aims, I argue, include the production of artefacts and culture through design processes, and not simply their reproduction through what is usually termed reconstruction. This language of occlusion is made increasingly entrenched through the desire to make each practice more exclusive, more professional. Moreover the chronotope may be used as a tool for making reconstructions; in an otherwise straightforwardly chronological review of drawing types and instruments, specific resemblances or tropes are identified regardless of their place in time or chronological sequence.

Organised across a four-and-a-half-metre long fold-out Chronotopic Chart (see Fig. 8) are a number of these "fleshed out"[195] moments. The Chart has *inter alia* enabled the analysis and development of the category of the 'undisciplined' already set out above and suggests chronotopic connections between other categories not yet developed. These chronotopes (including the undisciplined types), with one exception described below, are numbered 1 to 11. This is not an exhaustive list; it simply marks the point at which the density of the Chart began to make its use unwieldy. Indeed, the eleven chronotopes selected may already have exceeded that condition.

The Chronotopic Chart is ordered chronologically beginning at the top with the earliest (though contested) instance of an orthographic plan,[196] and concludes at the bottom with images made using near-contemporary 3d C.A.D. software (Fig. 9). Along the left-hand side are texts describing chronotopic categories whose original colour-coding relates to the highlighted images in the body of the chart. The images might, broadly and in columns, be categorised into; drawing instrument, drawing and event. Earlier versions of the chart were sharply divided into these three columnar categories, but this division has softened in subsequent versions as images have shifted, the better to graphically connect them whilst retaining a minimum degree of legibility. However, broadly, from left to right, these categories still obtain. Across the Chart, therefore, the occurrence of conditions pertaining to each discipline through 'events' – for example, the statutes or charters to which that discipline is subject – and the consequent professionalisation of that discipline, including drawings which reflect particular attitudes both internal and external to the discipline, is mapped against the kinds of drawing being made and used at that time, but also against the set of graphic conventions and projection types available (or allowable). The Chart may be further used to examine how these parallel developments in tools, techniques and practice reflect and influence those aims of architecture and archaeology that are professed and, at the same time, occluded, in particular how, in this account, these are reflected in the curious history, and pre-history, of London Stone.

I envisage that additionally the Chart could be used to test the hypothesis of the interconnectedness of tool, technique and event. It will be employed to investigate the claim that the centralising aims and protectionism of design professions, as professions, including archaeology, with all the legal paraphernalia associated with professionalisation, have not gone uncontested. The Chart may be used to explore the idea that the less readily politically controllable developmental trajectory of the tools of architecture and archaeology, have significantly influenced professional structures. This nexus of influences has, I would argue, had a profound effect on the status and presence of London Stone (and other such *sui generis* artefacts); a professionalised discipline with a policed centre makes no allowance, provides no space, for the uncategorisable, the taboo, the scandalous.

The selection of images used is highly partial. They represent that set of images which I had consulted in the pursuit of my research up to a certain point when I conceived (a quite different looking, tabular, version) of this chart as a method of both storing those imagesand then using them to construct narratives through them.

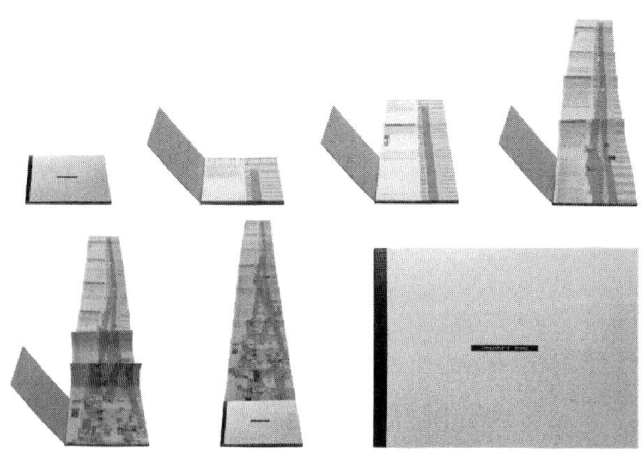

Fig. 8 Alessandro Zambelli, Chronotopic Reconstruction [photograph of fold-out chart - version originally printed for the Moves of London Stone tour]. 2013, Inkjet on paper, bound in cardboard, 445.5 x 42 cm.

Fig. 9 [opposite] Alessandro Zambelli, Chronotopic Reconstruction [full chart]. 2015, digital version.

CHRONOTOPIC CHART

Key and Image References

> Chronotopic reconstructions are mappings of discrete instances of temporal 'thickening' accompanied by spatial 'changing' 'responsive' to that thickening – that is, time thickened with 'plot and history.'

The drawing tools of architecture and archaeology, the drawings made with them and the professionalising events which have shaped those disciplines, may be used as chronotopic devices to calibrate the divergent practices of their parent disciplines, revealing alternative narratives of the development of those disciplines.

Except for those indicated as having been developed further in the body of the thesis (8, 9 and 10), these chronotopes are 'sketched-in' here only.

1. **Undisciplined Drawing: The Unfolded/Dissected Drawing**
   A form of orthographic projection - a panoptic view of all parts, especially those hidden, revealed simultaneously.
2. **False Friends**
   Highly local depictions of plan forms whose function is lost to us.
3. **The Reflexive Drawing #1**
   The image of the 'creative genius' is generally tied to the 'hand' and the 'tools' of that genius. Often these images of architects or antiquaries and their instruments are made by other architects or antiquaries.
4. **Undisciplined Drawing: Continuous Narrative**
   Passage of time and space as a series of sequential experiences are all depicted simultaneously.
5. **The Ruling Pen**
   Not a drawing type, but a cross-disciplinary drawing instrument, the ruling pen dominated mark-making in technical drawing for at least two thousand years until the mid twentieth-century, but now occupies only a small niche in the panoply of modern, largely software based, drawing instruments.
6. **The Occasional Rise of Automation**
   Periodically the drive to automate drawing processes gives rise to the generation of particular projection types.
7. **The Reflexive Drawing #2**
   Growing self-awareness and pride in the mastery of ones own discipline made for a different kind of reflexive drawing.
8. **Undisciplined Drawing: The 'Multi-informational Image'** (#1 in *3. Undiscipline*)
9. **Undisciplined Drawing: The Mise-en-Scène** (#2 in *3. Undiscipline*)
10. **Undisciplined Drawing: The Exploded Drawing** (#3 in *3. Undiscipline*)
11. **Tools of Pre-obsolescence**
   The manufacture of traditional drawing instruments or the continued development of traditional drawing instruments continues after their effective obsolescence. Or, with SketchUp for example a mimicking of traditional (though not necessarily obsolete) drawing techniques.

Date Ranges

6000-5951

5950-5901

5900-5851

5850-5801

5800-5751

5750-5701

5700-5651

5650-5601

5600-5551

5550-5501

5500-5451

5450-5401

5400-5351

5350-5301

5300-5251

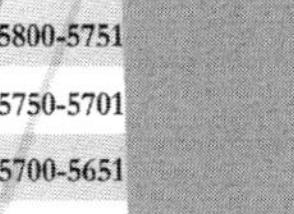

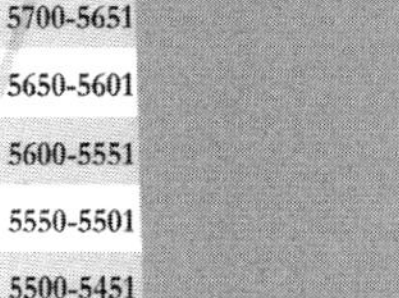

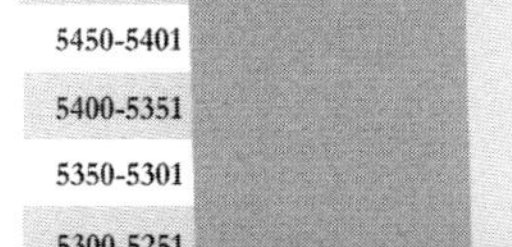

1 Undisciplined Drawing:
The Unfolded/Dissected Drawing

2 False Friends

5250-5201
5200-5151
5150-5101
5100-5051
5050-5001
5000-4951
4950-4901
4900-4851
4850-4801
4800-4751
4750-4701
4700-4651
4650-4601
4600-4551
4550-4501
4500-5451
4450-4401
4400-4351
4350-4301
4300-4251
4250-5201
4200-4151
4150-4101

3850-3801
3800-3751
3750-3701
3700-3651
3650-3601
3600-3551
3550-3501
3500-3451
3450-3401
3400-3351
3350-3301
3300-3251
3250-3201
3200-3151
3150-3101
3100-3051
3050-3001
3000-2951
2950-2901
2900-2851
2850-2801
2800-2751
2750-2701

3 The Reflexive Drawing #1

2700-2651

2650-2601

2

2600-2551

2550-2501

2500-2451

2450-2401

2400-2351

2350-2301

2300-2251

2250-2201

2200-2151

2150-2101

2000-1951

1950-1901

1900-1851

1850-1801

1800-1751

1750-1701

1700-1651

1650-1601

1600-1551

1550-1501

1500-1451

1450-1401

4 Undisciplined Drawing:
Continuous Narrative

1400-1351
1350-1301
1300-1251
1250-1201
1200-1151
1150-1101
1100-1051
1050-1001
1000-951
950-901
900-851
850-801

5 The Ruling Pen

700-651

650-601

600-551

550-501

ἀρχιτέκτων

500-451

450-401

400-351

350-301

300-251

250-201

200-151

150-101

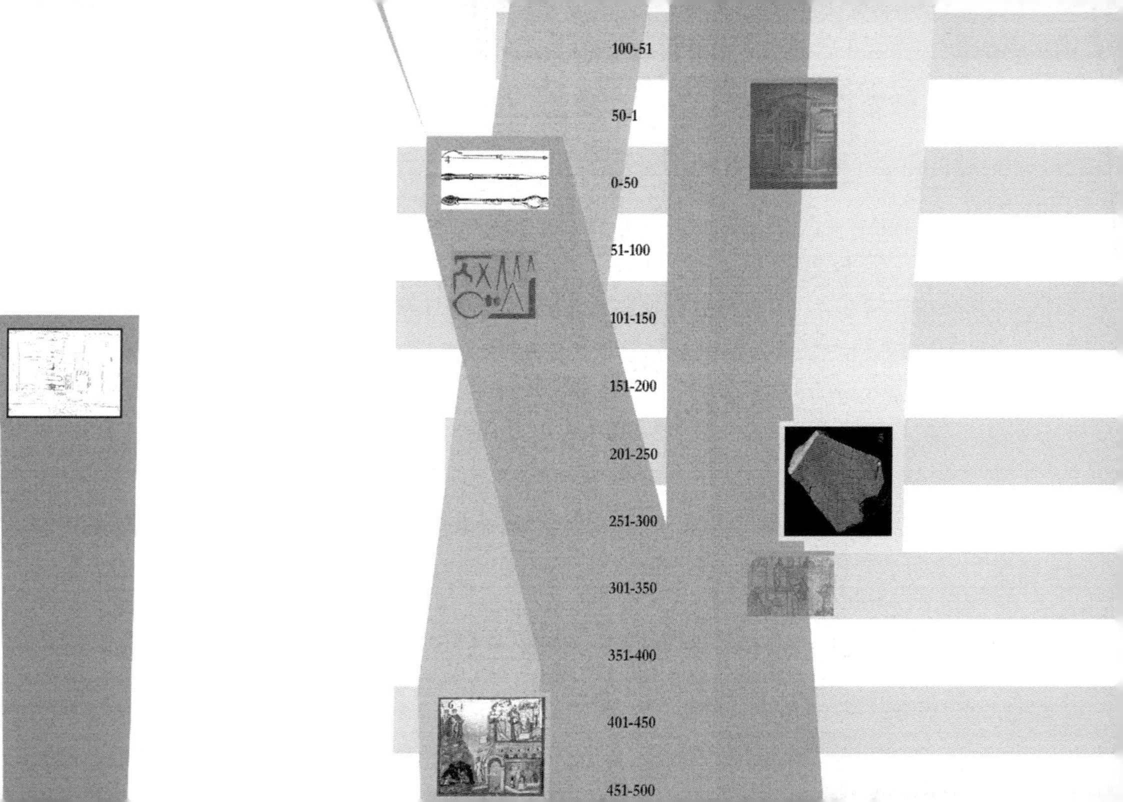
100-51
50-1
0-50
51-100
101-150
151-200
201-250
251-300
301-350
351-400
401-450
451-500

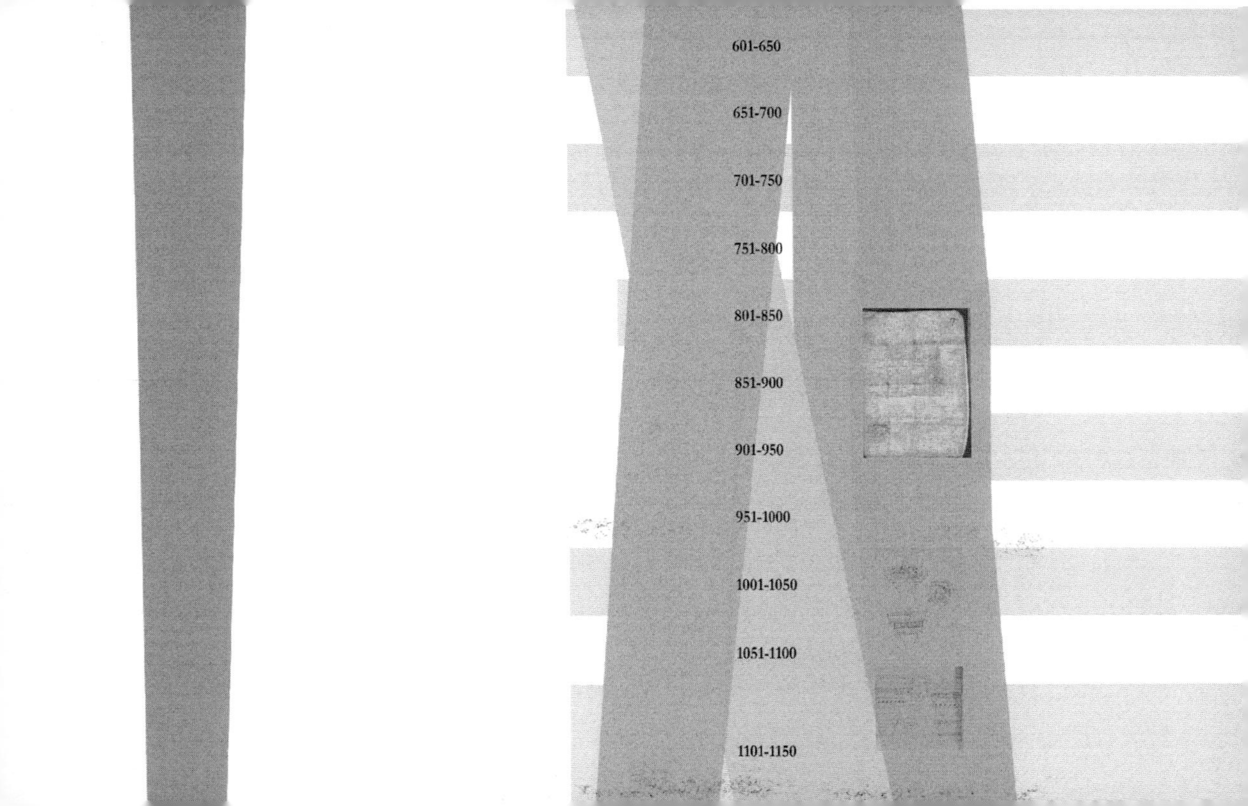
601-650
651-700
701-750
751-800
801-850
851-900
901-950
951-1000
1001-1050
1051-1100
1101-1150

6 The Occasional Rise of Automation

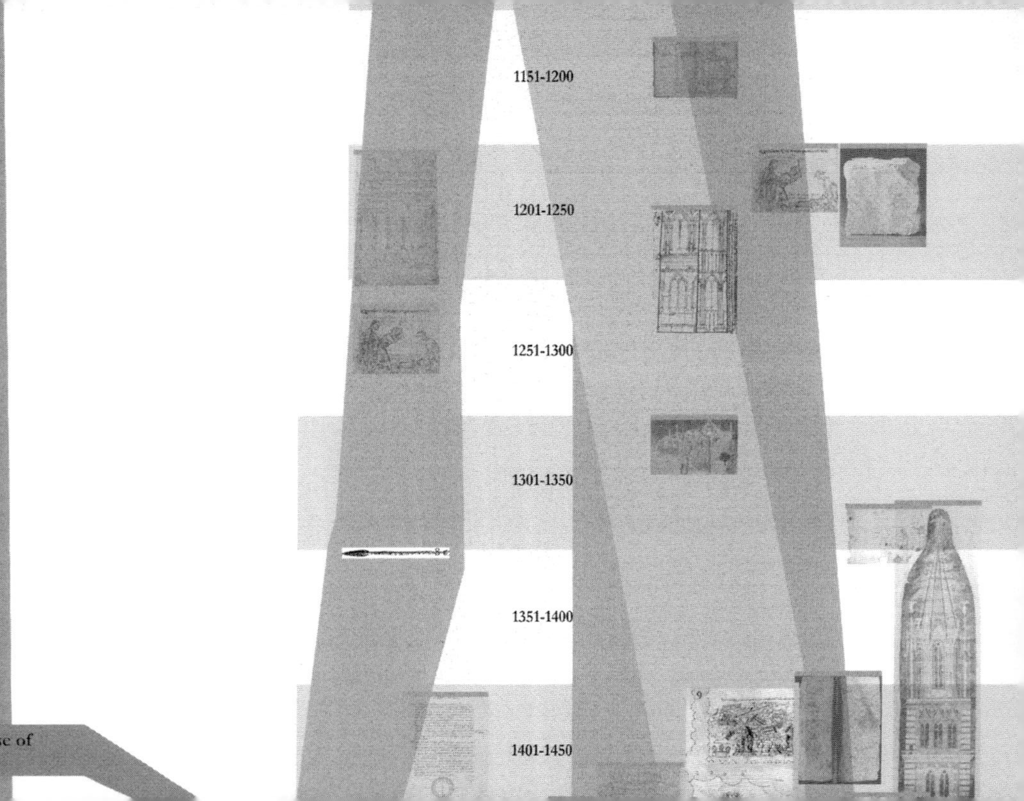

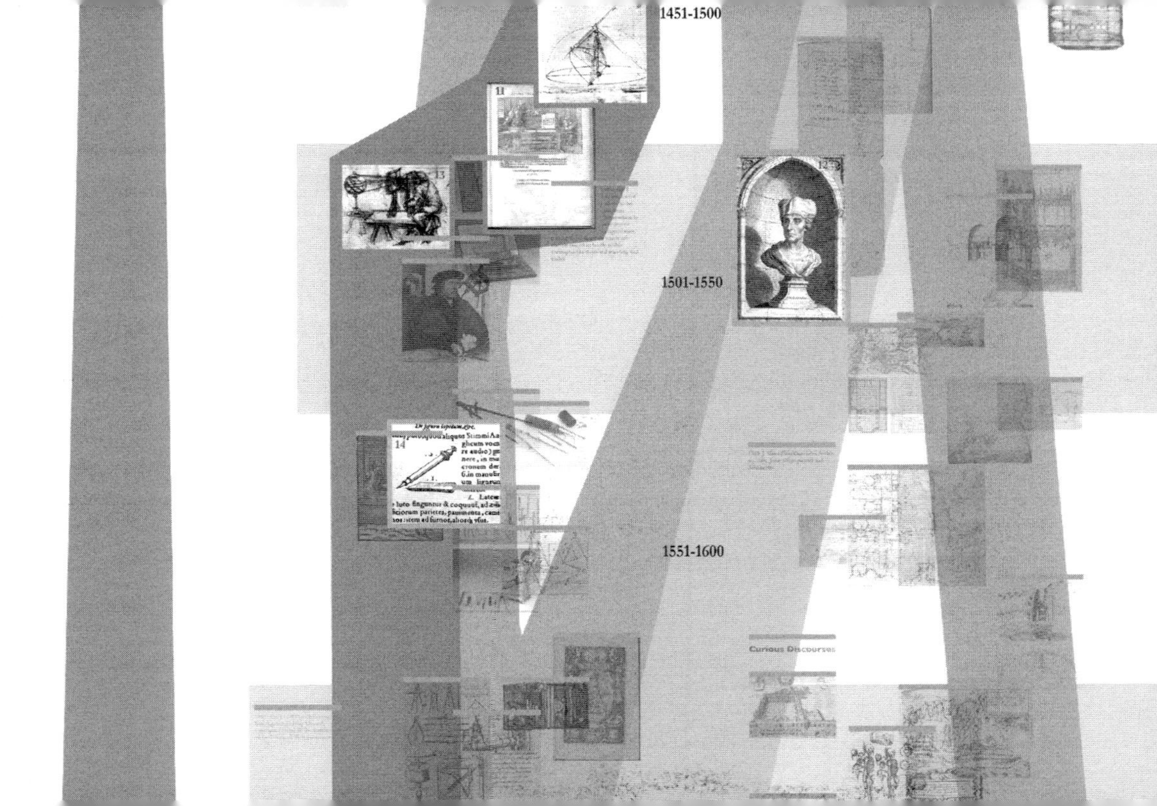
1451-1500
1501-1550
1551-1600
Curious Discourses

7 Undisciplined Drawing: The 'Multi-informational Image'
8 The Reflexive Drawing #2
1601-1650
1651-1700
1701-1750
15
16
17
18
19
20
21
22
23
24
26
27
29

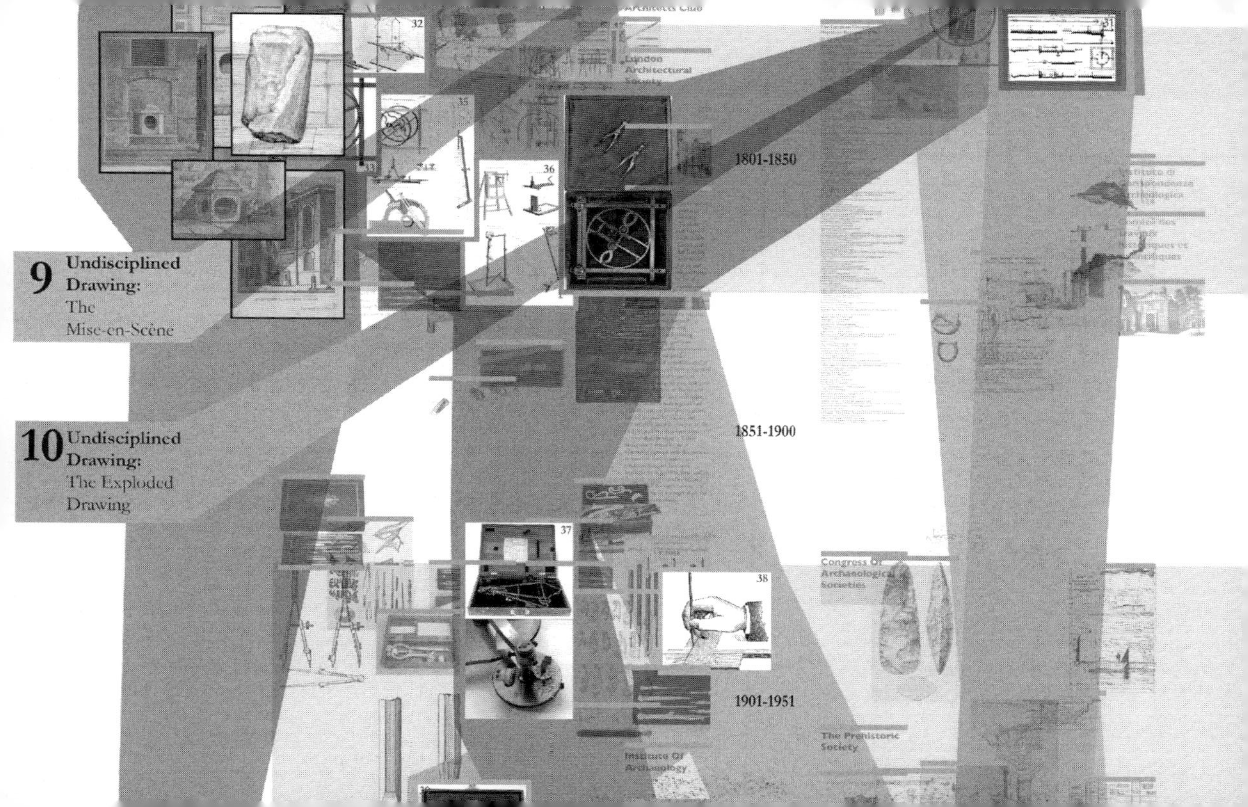

9 Undisciplined Drawing: The Mise-en-Scène
10 Undisciplined Drawing: The Exploded Drawing
1801-1850
1851-1900
1901-1951
London Architectural Society
Congress Of Archaeological Societies
The Prehistoric Society
Institute Of Archaeology
31
32
33
35
36
37
38

11 Tools of Pre-obsolescence

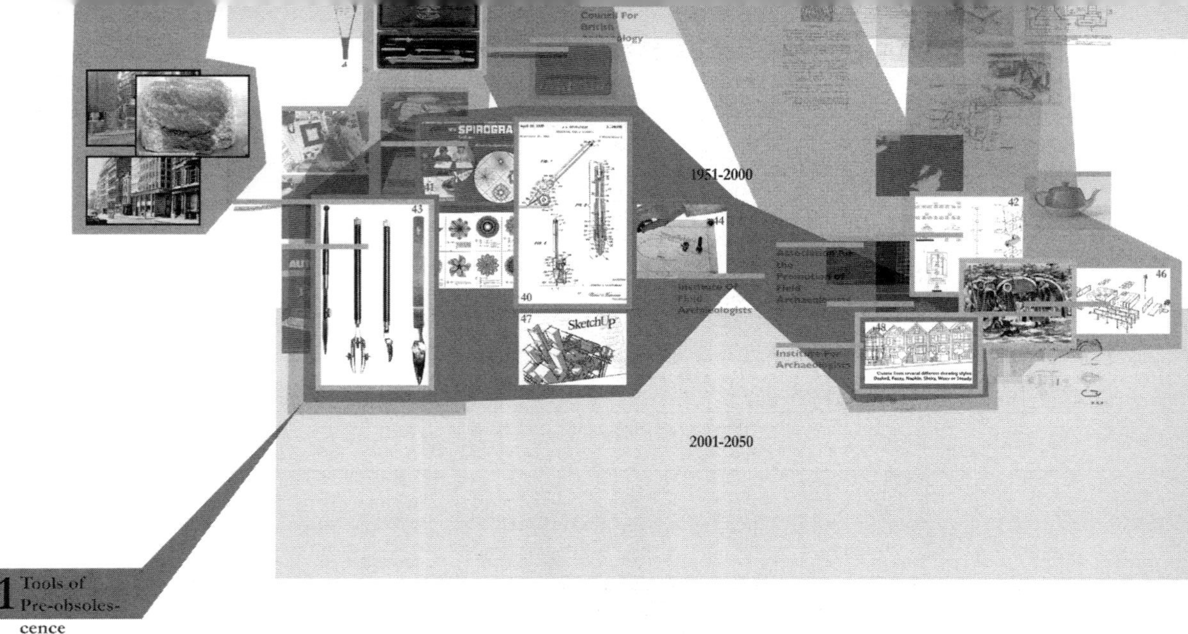

1

1 5900c Disputed town plan of Çatalhöyük though this may be a drawing of a leopard or a non-figurative pattern repeat (Meece 2006)- Orthogonal Plan- Neolithic Anatolia- Lavmen?- (Meece 2006)
3 1351-1334 Le dessin architectural chez les anciens Egyptiens, Badawy, 1948 101 -Domaine royal DAVIES, N. DE G.: "Amarna.", I, pl. XXXII.w
7 820c Plan of the Abbey of St Gall on calfskin "earliest architectural drawing of the western Middle Ages to survive" Kostof p.71- Orthogonal Plan- Ideal programmatic layout- Ackerman 2002:28- Kostof 1977:72- Image at http://www.stgallplan.org
26 1761 **'Section' of the Great Hall at Syon House, by Robert Adam, 1761**

2

1 5900c Disputed town plan of Çatalhöyük though this may be a drawing of a leopard or a non-figurative pattern repeat (Meece 2006)- Orthogonal Plan- Neolithic Anatolia- Lavmen?- (Meece 2006)
5 203-211 Forma Urbis Romae Plan of Rome on marble- Orthogonal Plan- Ancient Rome- Kostof 1977:52- Image at http://formaurbis.stanford.edu/fragments/color_mos_reduced/011d_MOS.jpg

3

2 2650-2600c In Egypt, the prototypical architect Imhotep was revered for his great wisdom as a scribe, astronomer, magician, and healer. As healer, he was later deified. Architecture for him represented one of the fields of learning he commanded, as well as the canvas of his cunning. Kostof 1977 p.3
12 1505-1552 John Leland The first person publicly to declare himself 'Antiquarius' or an antiquary was John Leland (c. 1505–1552) whose activities well exemplify the limitations of outlook in one who aspired to review the historical remains of England. He was a court scholar and priest who received a licence from King Henry VIII to search the monasteries and colleges throughout the country for rare and important manuscripts that could be removed to the King's own libraries. Thereafter he formed the ambition to travel the kingdom in order to give a comprehensive description of Britain, and made a 'Laborvouse Journey & Serche for Englandes Antiquitees' (fig. 15). The results – which he never published – were disappointing. Parry, Mists of Time
20 1731 Eighteenth century engraving showing a building under construction and the architect discussing some detail with his client. The accompanying verse is taken from Pope's Epistle to Lord Burlington. 1731. Mansell Collection. Drawing Instruments 1580-1980, Hambly M. 1988 p25
48 2002 Squiggle
'The Steady style looks like an architect's steady hand' Insight Development (San Ramon, 2002)

4

3 1351-1334 Le dessin architectural chez les anciens Égyptiens. Badawy, 1948 101 -Domaine royal DAVIES, N. DE G.: "Amarna.", I, pl. XXXII.w
6 5th Cent. The Discovery of the Past: the origins of archaeology, 1996, Schnapp A, p38 Aeneas at the construction of Carthage, a fifth century miniature. For the illustrator of the Vatican Virgil the building of Carthage belonged to the cycle of the invention of the arts. The image of the foundation of a town is rare in antique art. Here, the heroes Aeneas and Achates watch the construction of the city.
9 1400-1430c The Discovery of the Past: the origins of archaeology, 1996, Schnapp A, p115 The ruins of Troy, sketch from a manuscript by Cristoforo Buondelmonti, fifteenth century. A Florentine cleric, Buondelmonti was one of the most adventurous antiquaries of the fifteenth century: for sixteen years he travelled throughout the Greek islands, illustrating his manuscripts with maps and sketches of the most notable sites.
17 1645c The Invisible College
The beginnings of the Royal Society came about around 1645 when a group of scientists began to hold regular meetings. The common theme among the scientists who began the Society was acquiring knowledge by experimental investigation. The first group of such men included Robert Moray, Robert Boyle, John Wilkins, John Wallis, John Evelyn, Christopher Wren and William Petty.
Boyle, in his letters written in 1646 and 1647, refers to our Invisible College or the Philosophical College. In an October 1646 letter written to his former tutor Isaac Marcombe in Paris he says (see for example [6]):
The best of it is that the cornerstones of the Invisible (or as they term themselves the Philosophical) College, do now and then honour me with their company, which makes me sorry for those pressing occasions that urge my departure
In the regular meetings, Boyle writes, members of the College discussed:
... natural philosophy, the mechanics and husbandry according to the principles of the Philosophical College, that values no knowledge but that it has a tendency to use
http://www-history.mcs.st-and.ac.uk/Societies/RS.htm.

5

4 Roman Drawing Instruments 1580-1980, Hambly M. 1988 p58 Roman ruling pens. The simplest were made of lead bent over; others were of bronze with twin blades and a moveable ring to adjust the thickness of the lines drawn; some included a charcoal-stick holder at the other end. Roman Collection, Museum, Bonn
8 1515c Drawing Instruments 1580-1980, Hambly M. 1988 p58 Ruling pen, known to be Dürer's, since it was found behind a skirting board in his house in Nuremberg; steel with a tapered handle and with twin blades adjusted by a heavy sliding ring to alter the thickness of lines drawn. c. 1515. Germanisches Nationalmuseum, Nuremberg
14 1565 Drawing Instruments 1580-1980, Hambly M. 1988 p66 Earliest illustration of a pencil, a wood encased graphite stick, provided with moveable metal holder. Woodcut from Conrad Gesner's De omni rerum fossilium genere (Zurich, 1565).
Holding a ruling pen
39 1940-60c Set belonging to George McHugh, Engineer
A. G. Thornton Ltd. Techset. Mid-20th century.
43 1980c Drawing Instruments 1580-1980, Hambly M. 1988 p63
Late-20th-century specialist drawing pens by Haff all with plain ebonite handles, the blades made of stainless steel with hardened tips. (Right to left): Broad pen with numbered settings on a thumb-screw from 0.25-1.20 mm thick; a curve line pen for lines 0.1-0.35 mm thick; a twin road or rail pen; a small fine-line pen for lines 0.2-0.8 mm thick. c.1980.

6

10 1452-1519 c Drawing Instruments 1580-1980, Hambly M. 1988 p98 An early method of setting up a parabolic curve, as drawn by Leonardo da Vinci in a notebook now in the Ambrosiana Library, Milan.
11 1494 Summa de arithmetica, geometria, proportioni et proportionalita, published by Luca Pacioli (1445-1509) in 1494
13 1510 Architectural Representation and the Perspective Hinge, Perez-Gomez A & Pelletier L. 1997 p31 A sketch by Leonardo da Vinci shows a draftsman drawing an armillary sphere with the help of a transparent plane (ca. 1510). This is a rare example showing Leonardo's interest in linear perspective.
15 1630-1640c Architectural Representation and the Perspective Hinge, Perez-Gomez A & Pelletier L. 1997 p145 Drawing Instruments 1580-1980, Hambly M. 1988 p146 Engraving from Bion's Mathematische Werkschule which illustrates (fig.1) Benjamin Bramer's table apparatus, of c.1630, with two sighting pin-holes at (A) and (B) and a timber drawing frame (D-G and E-F). Fig.3 shows the apparatus designed by Jean F. Niceron, a French mathematician and optician. c.1640
18 1669 Drawing Instruments 1580-1980, Hambly M. 1988 p147
Engraving from Mathematische Werkschule (a German version of Bion), which illustrates (fig. I) the perspectograph designed by Sir Christopher Wren in 1669. Fig.5 shows another apparatus which has two viewing points and operates with a horizontal drawing parallel motion.
27 1760 Drawing Instruments 1580-1980, Hambly M. 1988 p97
Volute compasses in silver made for George III and signed 'D. Lyle 1760'. These consist of a beam divided into inches similar to a beam compass, but with a helical drum unit fixed to the plane of the beam. A catgut thread connects the end of the helical curved spring to the pencil-holder. The beam is rotated with the centre fixed, and the drawing point traces a spiral curve. Alternative helical drums are included in the shagreen-covered fitted case for drawing different spiral curves. Beam length 7½in (190 mm). George III Collection, Science Museum, London.
28 1763 Drawing Instruments 1580-1980, Hambly M. 1988 p131
Pantograph shown in use, as illustrated in the Dessein section of the Encyclopédie of Diderot & d'Alembert, published in Paris in 1763.
29 1765 Drawing Instruments 1580-1980, Hambly M. 1988 p148
Perspective apparatus designed by the engineer James Watt and made by him in Glasgow in 1765. This is an ingenious device, easily transportable, for use in external perspectives. The apparatus folds away into a fitted hardwood case, which also forms the drawing board; its stand fits together to form a walking stick. Science Museum, London
30 1790c Drawing Instruments 1580-1980, Hambly M. 1988 p90
Ellipsograph of brass and steel inscribed 'Gourdin à Paris' with frame and circular plate designed as a trammel slotted to take the drawing arm; the four adjustable feet at the corners are missing. c.1790. Museum of the History of Science, Oxford
31 1793-1794 Making Things the Same: Representation, Tolerance and the End of the Ancien Regime in France, 1998, Alder K.
From Monge's Description de l'art de fabriquer les canons (1793-94) shows an 'exploded' view of the main precision instrument for measuring the interior diameter of the canon bore. Note the use of the centimetre scale, which had only that year come into use.
32 1796 Drawing Instruments 1580-1980, Hambly M. 1988 p148
Engraving from George Adams the Younger's Geometrical and Graphical Essays dated December 1796. Fig 2 shows Adams' perspective apparatus . . . which incorporates three rollers to operate the drawing point suspended by wires from a counter-balanced metal frame
33 1813 Drawing Instruments 1580-1980, Hambly M. 1988 p91
Ellipsograph designed by John Farey inscribed 'Farey Invt London'; a prototype similar to this was awarded a Gold Medal by the Society of Arts in 1813. Private collection.
34 1815c Drawing Instruments 1580-1980, Hambly M. 1988 Plate V
Ellipsograph inscribed 'Farey London No 22' shown in its original fishskin covered case lined with velvet, complete with a pair of miniature bow compasses, one for pencil, one for ink. Case: 7x7 in (178mm). English, c.1815. RIBA Collection, London
36 1819 Drawing Instruments 1580-1980, Hambly M. 1988 p149
John Farey's plate illustrating Delineators from Dr Abraham Rees' Cyclopaedia (1819)
37 1890-1900
This integrator is the most sophisticated form [of planimeter], with three recording mechanisms, giving the area, moment, and moment of inertia. It is also the extra large model, only made to special order. Running on a 78 inch rail, it has a longitudinal reach of 67 inches, and transverse reach of 26 inches. It is complete (apart from the rail), and in full working order
Private, Switzerland
http://www.theglass.com/index.php?a=2&b=4942
40 1965
United States Patent Office 3,179,089, Patented Apr. 20, 1965
The present invention relates to pencils and more particularly to mechanical pencils of the type used in engineering drafting.
In pencilling engineering drawings and the like, it is highly desirable to manually rotate the pencil while drawing a line to keep the pencil point sharp for a longer period of time. The practice of manually rotating

McCarthy and Nurse, Making History: Antiquaries in Britain, 1707-2007
22 1756 Il Mausoleo di Ottaviano, Giambatista Piranesi
Giovanni Battista Piranesi and Francesco Piranesi, Le Antichità Romane, Opere Di Giambatista Piranesi

8

19 1719-1720 Architectural Representation and the Perspective Hinge, Perez-Gomez A & Pelletier L, 1997 p50
Johann Jacob Schübler, Perspectiva Pes Picturae (1719-1720)
. . . demonstrates how clearly the homology of plan, elevation, and perspective was understood. Perspective had become the primary architectural idea, allowing for the conception of architectural space as a geometrized yet transcendental entity
20 1731 Eighteenth-century engraving showing a building under construction and the architect discussing some detail with his client. The accompanying verse is taken from Pope's Epistle to Lord Burlington. 1731. Mansell Collection. Drawing Instruments 1580-1980, Hambly M. 1988 p25
21 1740 Excavation of a Hypocaust at Lincoln, George Vertue,
McCarthy and Nurse, Making History: Antiquaries in Britain, 1707-2007.
22 1756 Il Mausoleo di Ottaviano, Giambatista Piranesi
Giovanni Battista Piranesi and Francesco Piranesi, Le Antichità Romane, Opera Di Giambatista Piranesi

9

24 1760 Piranesi Arch Trajan Benevento
45 1976 Man Before History: The Making of the Past John Waechter

10

31 1793-1794 Making Things the Same: Representation, Tolerance and the End of the Ancien Regime in France, 1998, Alder K.
From Monge's Description de l'art de fabriquer les canons (1793-94) shows an 'exploded' view of the main precision instrument for measuring the interior diameter of the canon bore. Note the use of the centimetre scale, which had only that year come into use.
42 1979 Principles of archaeological stratigraphy, 1979, Harris E.
The compilation of a stratigraphic sequence. In (A) all the superpositional relationships are shown in the section and in the Harris Matrix form. (B) A matrix rendition of a section, which is clarified into a stratigraphic sequence in (C), according to the Law of Stratigraphical Succession.
46 1978 Rogers Autonomous House

11

40 1965
United States Patent Office, 3,179,089, Patented Apr. 20, 1965
The present invention relates to pencils and more particularly to mechanical pencils of the type used in engineering drafting.
In pencilling engineering drawings and the like, it is highly desirable to manually rotate the pencil while drawing a line to keep the pencil point sharp for a longer period of time. This practice of manually rotating the pencil in addition to reducing the frequency at which the pencil requires resharpening, provides clean-cut lines of uniform thickness to improve the appearance of the drawing
41 1965 The Spirograph . . . was developed by the British engineer Denys Fisher, who exhibited it in 1965 at the Nuremberg International Toy Fair. It was subsequently produced by his company. US distribution rights were acquired by Kenner, Inc., which introduced it to the United States market in 1966, promoting it as a creative children's toy. [Wikipedia]
43 1980c Drawing Instruments 1580-1980, Hambly M. 1988 p63
Late-20th-century specialist drawing pens by Haff all with plain ebonite handles, the blades made of stainless steel with hardened tips. (Right to left): Broad pen with numbered settings on a thumb-screw from 0.25-1.20 mm thick; a curve line pen for lines 0.1-0.35 mm thick; a twin road or rail pen; a small fine-line pen for lines 0.2-0.8 mm thick. c.1980.
44 1980c Drawing Instruments 1580-1980, Hambly M. 1988 p95
Ellipsograph by Haff in transparent acrylic sheet with chrome plated rotating operating knobs, for use with either ink, pencil or a technical pen. The semi-axes of the ellipse are set using two engraved scales. After the drawing point has been inserted and lowered into position the ellipse can be drawn in one complete movement simply by rotating the knob on the upper circle. Small version 6¾ x 4 in (170 x 116mm)
47 2000 SketchUp Drawing on a Napkin.
www.sketchup.com accessed via waybackmachine http://web.archive.org/web/20020402092147/http://www.sketchup.com/ on 14.2.13
"SketchUp is a deceptively simple, amazingly powerful tool for creating, viewing, and modifying 3D ideas quickly and easily. It has been developed to combine the elegance and spontaneity of pencil sketching with the speed and flexibility of today's digital media. SketchUp enhances your creativity and productivity."
SketchUp v2 April 2002
48 2002 Squiggle
'The Steady style looks like an architect's steady hand' Insight Development (San Ramon, 2002)

My use of the term 'chronotope' to describe these narrative groupings came later. Very few images were added after the date above and this 'artificial' cut-off date is reflected in the fact that, for example, the 'undisciplined' chronotopes developed in the body of this account include more, and different, images to those found in the Chart which spawned them.

The chronotopic bands were coloured quickly and to aid legibility. The shapes of the bands were also drawn rapidly and adjusted only to aid the visibility of the images themselves.[197] Many images are partially obscured but, since the purpose of the Chart was, foremost, to aid the making of chronotopic connections, obscured images could, in its electronic version, be quickly revealed and the references for those images accessed. To the left of the Chart is an unnamed, grey-coloured, chronotope containing key representations of London Stone. This was added late in the process of constructing the Chart and, although the addition of this narrative is, in retrospect, an obvious, even inevitable, move, it, and its connection to the other images, remains largely unexplored.

Choreographic Reconstruction

Although the extraordinary ordinariness of London Stone is central to its story, the 'choreographic' here is not Allan Pred's all-encompassing, "choreography of existence"[198] but owes more to William Forsythe's observation that, "historically choreography has been indivisible from the human body in action"[199] but that now, for him, "choreography and dancing are two distinct and very different practices" and then asks "is it possible for choreography to generate autonomous expressions of its principles, a choreographic object, without the body [...] What else, besides the body, could physical thinking look like?"[200]

London Stone is now approximately eighteen meters from its probable, original, Roman location having moved at least six times since its foundation. It is also six metres above Roman street level, a datum coinciding almost exactly with the floors of the underground trains passing directly below. A choreographic reconstruction maps these presences, absences and movements and the changing of the Stone's various contexts chronologically. By the time of its first written mention in the early tenth or possibly early, but more likely late, twelfth-century in connection with either Æthelstan, King of England or Henry Fitz Ailwin, the first mayor of London, respectively,[201] it had found itself surrounded on all sides by the ever-widening Cannon Street. A hazard to traffic, the Stone was first encased in the seventeenth-century. Burned and reduced in the Great Fire it was moved, and moved again, bombed and then moved twice more, ultimately to be put behind glass and grille and most recently just glass.

Over the centuries a loose and largely oral collection of folkloric fragments began to cleave to it, culminating in 1882 with what became a much repeated mythic fabrication tying the fate of the Stone to the fate of the City and their (Stone and city) origins in Brutus's flight from Troy.[202] As the myths grew so the Stone gradually disappeared from view, hidden in plain sight. Forgotten and displaced, it had become, and remains until its most recent move in 2018, all but invisible. It is the very invisibility of London Stone, the accidental removal of its "ocularcentrism"[203] which I attempt to recover for the visual and recast through the re-enactment of its choreography and through the performance of the texts which have become its contexts.

In 2006 in *The Uses of Heritage*, Laurajane Smith coined the term "authorized heritage discourse"[204] to describe how discussion surrounding issues of heritage is commonly and normatively used to "naturalize certain ideas about the immutable and inherent nature of the value and meaning of heritage."[205] Instead, what heritage should be doing, according to Smith, "is intersect with a range of values and identities, and subsequently play a part in their validation, negotiation and regulation,"[206] and that, "the process or moment of heritage is [...]

critically active and self-conscious."[207] *The Moves of London Stone* tour, through a short guided walk, attempts to engage, therefore, in a "critically active" register – not directly with its misplaced, occluded object, the Stone itself – but with its movements or, as Tim Brennan might term them, its "manoeuvres."[208] Simultaneously this 'tour' takes as central Phil Smith's view of heritage space (just, as we have seen above, with Shank's view of archaeological space) that it is "always in the process of being produced."[209]

Smith identifies three broad categories of arts-practice-based walking; the "European psychogeographical 'drift,'" the largely American class of "landscape interventions," and a tradition derived from "the rise of non-functional walking in Europe in the late eighteenth and early nineteenth century,"[210] which he situates within the Romantic movement. Furthermore, according to Smith the 'drift' category is "the principal touchstone"[211] for all other categories, reaching its apogee in the mid-twentieth-century "ludic" urban practices of the Lettrists and Situationists. This ludic tradition is preserved, he argues, in the pyschogeographic touring of Will Self and Iain Sinclair. A tradition maintained, he further argues, in contemporary participatory walking and touring practices, exemplified by Townley and Bradby,[212] Carl Lavery and Dee Heddon (Smith's erstwhile collaborators),[213] and in the work of Gail Burton, Serena Korda and Clare Qualmann,[214] all reifiers of the everyday. More pertinently, perhaps, for my performance of *The Moves of London Stone* is the highly structured, observational and, I would argue, much more politically motivated work of Francis Alÿs in his Seven Walks[215] suite of projects, in the fictional dramas of Janet Cardiff's "audio walks,"[216] but also in Jane Rendell's scripted plays of interwoven casts of the living, dead and fictional in *Walking Backwards through Brassaï* and in *Walking to Wapping/Walking through Angels*.[217] The sense of the bathetic, important in *The Moves of London Stone* tour might alternatively also find its origins in, as Smith describes it, the "substitution of quotidian for iconic space and a riffing on the tropes of the guiding script," in Fluxus-organised tours, in the mid-1970s, of "neglected" New York, satirically performed by Yoko Ono, Nam June Paik and others.[218]

My performance of, *The Moves of London Stone*, was a critical guided tour which took place during the afternoon of Friday, 18 October, 2013 (Fig. 10) and whose object was the bathetic re-enactment of the Stone's on-going, imperceptibly slow (and highly local) journey.

Following Brennan this "manoeuvre" or "walk-work of imagination"[219] was a "manipulation of the guided-walk form."[220] Specifically, this "discursive

Fig. 10 Alessandro Zambelli, The Moves of London Stone tour [invitation]. 2013, Digital and inkjet print on paper.

to targeted groups of participant walkers at various intervals."[221] Though involving less audience participation than Brennan's work typically does, and certainly less than the extreme participatory strategies of Townley and Bradby,[222] it very much adhered to Brennan's notion and desire that the "collision of textual fragments [...] conspire to arrive as the cultural surfacings of a place."[223]

The following text, therefore, was performed by me, accompanied by my invited guests, during *The Moves of London Stone* tour. The images are either from the tour booklet I distributed amongst the participants, or were exhibited at the Guildhall Library immediately after the tour.

PRELUDE: ORIGINS TO ENCASEMENT

It will be remembered that the other day an effort was made to "move on" Mrs. Rebecca Daisy, the old woman who keeps a sweetstuff stall on the pavement close to St. Swithin's Church, in Cannon Street.[224] __________

The Stone before the Fire of London, was much worn away, and as it were but a Stump remaining. But is now for the Preservation of it cased over with a new Stone handsomely wrought, cut hollow underneath so as the old Stone may be seen, the new one being over it, to shelter and defend the venerable one.[225] __________ *[...] some have supposed [it] to have been British; a stone, which might have been part of a Druidical circle, or some such other object of the ancient religion [...] Others have conjectured it to be a milliary stone [...]. It seems preserved like the Palladium of the city...*[226] __________ *London Stone may have only survived because it was the most important part of London's megalithic complex, the omphalos stone of the capital.*[227] __________

It is so sure a stone that that is upon sette,

For though some have it threttte

With Manases grym an grette

Yet hurte had it none:

Chryste is the very stone

That the citie is set uppon,

Which from al hys foone

Hath ever preserved yt.[228] __________

Can any of your scientific correspondents supply me with the geological character of the above stone, by far the most ancient monument in the city of London, and held by tradition to be its foundation stone?[229] __________ *It was [...] the altar of the Temple of Diana, on which the old British Kings took the oaths on their accession ...it was brought from Troy by*

Brutus, and laid down by his own hand as the altar-stone of the Diana Temple, the foundation stone of London and its palladium[230] _________ *[for] so long as the stone of Brutus is safe, so long shall London flourish*[231] _________ *When we were setting up the shop, there were cowboy builders here, and one of them was just about to take a chisel to the stone. I told him "Woah. Stop right there".*[232] _________

At length he sat on London Stone, & heard Jerusalem's voice.[233] _________

FIRST MOVEMENT (13th December 1742)

And she has seen many changes. [Mrs. Daisy] can remember the introduction of milk chocolate and the underground railway, and many other things.[234] __________

These, however, are but conjectures; nor can we say more, than that it is very singular, so much care should have been taken to preserve the stone, and so little to preserve the history of its origin.[235] __________ *On the south side of this high street, near unto the channel, is pitched upright a great stone called London stone, fixed in the ground very deep, fastened with bars of iron, and otherwise so strongly set, that if carts do run against it through negligence, the wheels be broken, and the stone itself unshaken.*[236] __________ *which I take to have beene a Milliarie, or Milemarke, such as was in the mercat place of Rome: From which was taken the dimension of all journeys every way, considering it is in the very mids of the City, as it lieth in length.*[237] __________ *foot of it laid in Rom. Mortar (so hard as the workmen could scarce in 3 days beat it thro) [...] 10′ deeper than the Roman level*[238] __________

Its foundations, which were uncovered during the operations which took place after the great fire, were found to be so extensive that Wren, who does not appear to have doubted that they were Roman, was inclined to think that they must have supported some more considerable monument[239] __________ *For before this it stood close to the edge of the kerb-stone on the same side of the street, to which it seems it had been removed from its original position on the opposite side in December 1742.*[240] __________ *That the Stone, commonly called London Stone, be placed against the Church, according to the churchwardens' discretion*[241] __________ *Under what innovating name can we term the cause that has removed the London-stone, in Cannon-street, the awful informant of the antiquity of this town, some yards more to the East of the church?*[242] __________

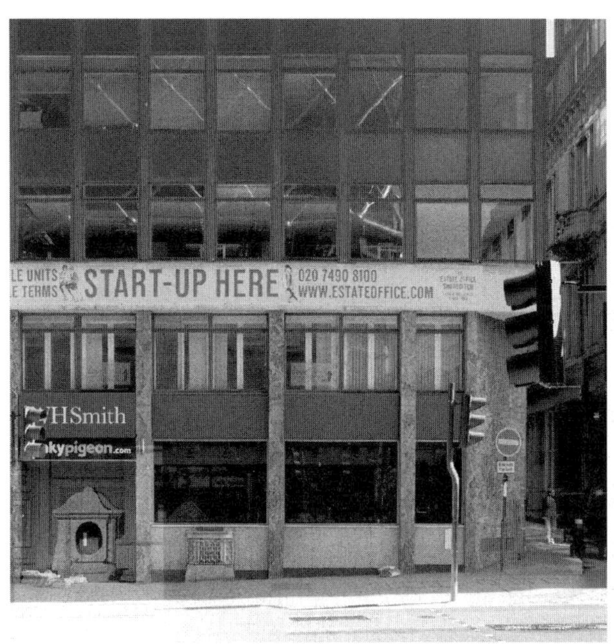

Fig. 11 Alessandro Zambelli, London Stone now and then. 2013, Digital photograph and photomontage. Overlaid image: N. Smith. London Stone in Cannon Street. 1791. London Metropolitan Archives.

SECOND MOVEMENT (1798-1801)

Mr. Thomas Marden, of Sherbourn Lane, printer, when that church was about to undergo a repair in 1798, prevailed on the parish-officers to consent that the stone should be placed where it still remains, after it had been doomed to destruction as a nuisance[243] _________

the Drapers man at London-stone

Was in your bed, and what sweet work he made

there.[244] _________ *Pray, Gentlemen, when was London Stone first Erected, and what was the design of its erection?*[245] _________

Soft I smell: Oh pure Nose.

Delio. Wat do you smell?

Frisc. I haue the scent of London-stone as full in my nose,

as Abchurch-lane of mother Walles Pasties: Sirrs feele a-

bout, I smell London-stone.

Alua. Wat be dis?[246] _________

Fig. 12 *Alessandro Zambelli, London Stone now and then. 2013, Digital photograph and photomontage. Overlaid image: Anon. The London Stone Street, 1801. London Metropolitan Archives.*

THIRD MOVEMENT (1801-1829, but probably in 1824)

The central division contains a large window with an arched head, the lateral divisions smaller windows of the same form, with elliptically arched doorways beneath them, the easternmost being walled up: below the central window is a hollow pedestal, containing the last fragment of the famous London stone[247] ___________

Fig. 13 Alessandro Zambelli, London Stone now and then. 2013, Digital photograph and photomontage. Overlaid image: J. Shury, St. Swithen, London Stone, c. 1825. London Metropolitan Archives.

INTERVAL: GRILLED (1869)

"Lor' love yer – yes," said Mrs Daisy.

Mrs. Daisy's stall is set up close beside what is probably the oldest piece of Old London now in existence. This is the Saxum Londiniense, or London Stone, a rounded block of stone of which a glimpse can be seen through the ornamental ironwork.[248] _________

LONG PLACED ABOVT XXXV FEET HENCE TOWARDS THE SOVTH WEST AND AFTERWARDS BVILT INTO THE WALL OF THIS CHVRCH WAS FOR MORE CAREFVL PROTECTION AND TRANSMISSION TO FVTVRE AGES BETTER SECURED BY THE CHVRCHWARDENS IN THE YEAR OF OVR LORD MDCCCLXIX.[249] _________ *While Los spoke, the terrible Spectre fell shudd'ring before him [...] Groaning he kneel'd before Los's iron-shod feet on London Stone,*[250] _________

FOURTH MOVEMENT (1961)

Fortunately for Mrs. Daisy, the Chief Commissioner of the City Police, Sir Henry Smith, refused to allow her to be sent away from the position she has held for so many years, and she therefore remains.[251] __________

thereafter the church shall be wholly demolished by the Board and the site thereof shall be sold, let or exchanged by the Board; provided that the monument known as London Stone, now incorporated in the south wall of the church, shall be carefully removed and preserved by the Board and re-erected as near as possible to its present site.[252] __________ *Dear Mr Cook... Thank you for your letter of the 22nd March. I will be very pleased to arrange to have the stone transported to the Museum in the Royal Exchange as soon as the demolition of the remains of the Church is commenced. I think that your suggestion to keep the stone until it is required on site is an excellent one, and you may rest assured that we shall endeavour to assist you in every way possible.*[253] __________

FIFTH MOVEMENT (October 1962)

Here begynneth the maryage of London Stone and the fayre pusell the bosse of Byllyngesgate.[254] __________ *and there he went around a great stone striking it with his sword, and there he set the three heads on a tower*[255] __________ *He rode thorough dyvers stretes of the cytie, and as he came by London stone, he strake it with his sworde, and sayd, "Nowe is Mortymer lorde of this cytie."*[256] __________

Enter Iacke Cade and the rest, and strikes his sword

vpon London stone.

Cade. Now is Mortemer Lord of this Citie,

And now sitting vpon London stone, We command,

That the first yeare of our raigne,

The pissing Cundit run nothing but red wine.[257] __________

Enter Iacke Cade and the rest, and strikes his

staffe on London stone.

Cade. Now is Mortimer Lord of this City,

And heere sitting vpon London Stone,

I charge and command, that of the Cities cost

The pissing Conduit run nothing but Clarret Wine

This first yeare of our raigne.[258] __________

by a jury were found badd and deceitful and by judgement of the Court condemned to be broken, defaced and spoyled both glasse and frame the which judgement was executed accordingly in Canning Street on the remayning parte of London Stone where the same were with a hammer broken all in pieces.[259] __________

Where Albion slept beneath the Fatal Tree,

And the Druids' golden Knife

Rioted in human gore,

In Offerings of Human Life?

They groan'd aloud on London Stone,[260] _________

and how I visited London Stone, and struck my staff upon it, in imitation of that arch rebel, Jack Cade.[261] _________ *There are one or two long cuts or indentations in the top, which are said to have been made by Jack Cade's sword, when he struck it against the stone*[262] _________

Cade. Fling all my dead Subjects into the Thames. Now say, what place is this?

Butcher. 'Tis London-Stone.[263] _________

following the completion of the new building on the site to house the Bank of China, the stone was placed without ceremony in the specially constructed grilled and glazed alcove that it occupies today.[264] _________

Fig. 14 Alessandro Zambelli, London Stone now and then. 2013, Digital photograph and photomontage. Overlaid image: Anon., 97-113 Cannon Street, 1969. London Metropolitan Archives.

It has no healing properties; it was not dropped or thrown by a giant, nor yet by the Devil; it is not a petrified dancer who profaned the Lord's Day. It is not 'countless', nor has it grown in size. It played no part in the death by hanging of a sheep stealer. It is not the haunt of fairies; it does not bring good luck or visions to those who walk round it three times; it does not go down to the Thames to drink when it hears the clock of St Swithin's church strike midnight, nor (apparently) has it ever resisted the efforts of a team of forty oxen to move it from its original site[265] __________

That, just now, is her strong point. [Mrs. Daisy] says she isn't going until she is removed in a narrow box – which shall not be more than twenty-four inches wide.[266] __________

Fig. 15 Alessandro Zambelli, London Stone now and then. 2013, Digital photograph and photomontage. Overlaid image: David Wright, Remains of St. Swithin's Church, 1962. The Geograph Britain and Ireland.

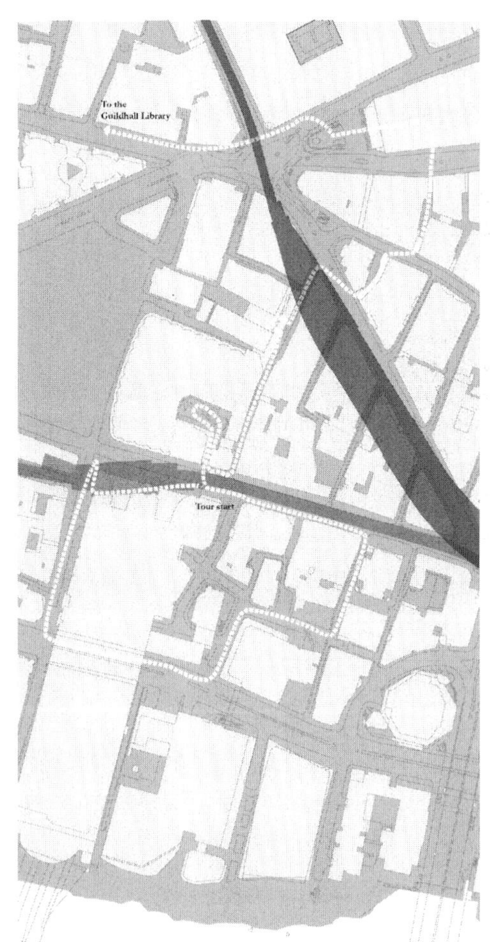

Fig. 16 Alessandro Zambelli, The Moves of London Stone tour route. 2015. Based upon: pdf map, Scale 1:500, Ordnance Survey, Mastermap, 2015. From: EDINA Digimap Ordnance Survey Service, http://edina.ac.uk/digimap.

That Friday afternoon, for a couple of hours, we moved with our invisible partners – not just London Stone but also with the ghostly company of those who have, or might have, accompanied it across the centuries: Brutus, Los, Henry Fitz Ailwin, Jack Cade, Rebecca Daisy, Chris Cheek - backwards and forwards, over and, at times, under Cannon Street. Figs. 16 and 17 record this intertwined dance producing a choreography of lightly scripted movement; walking and talking, reconstituting, reconstructing, re-making through analogical acts of offer and proposition.

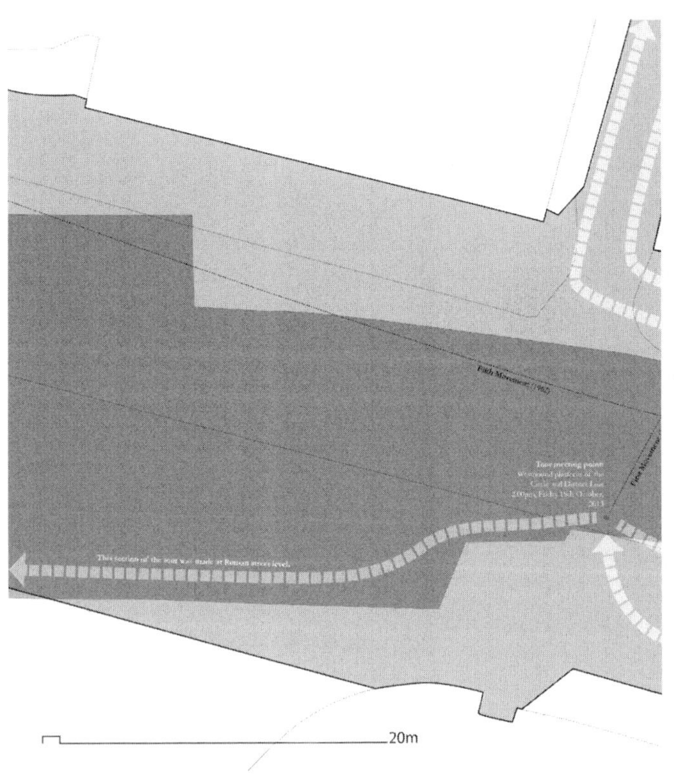

Fig. 17 The Moves of London Stone tour. Tour and Stone movements superimposed. 2015. Based upon: pdf map, Scale 1:500, Ordnance Survey, Mastermap, 2015. From: EDINA Digimap Ordnance Survey Service, http://edina.ac.uk/digimap.

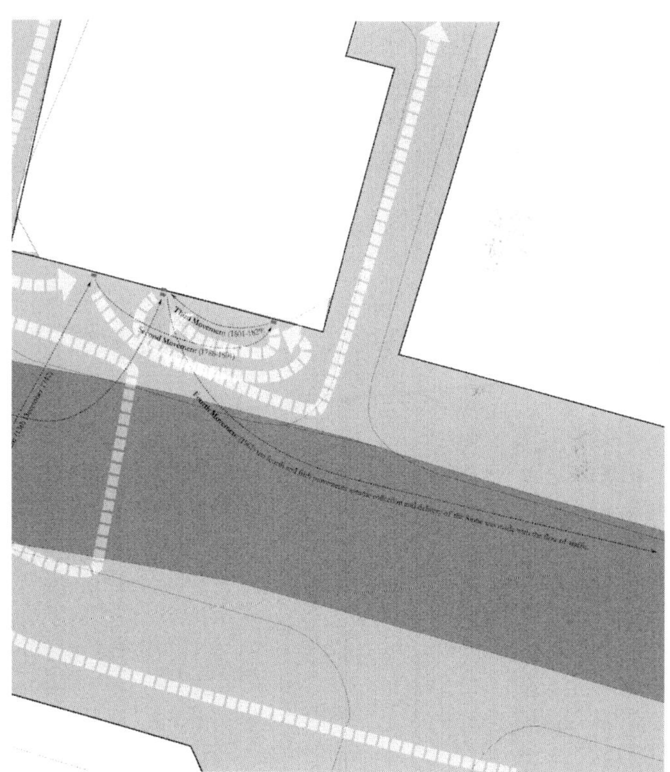
Third Movement
Second Movement
Fourth Movement

Instrumental Reconstruction

The homological relationship between architecture and archaeology is discernible in the resemblance between the aims of these two disciplines; specifically through processes of design and reconstruction and their products – drawings, excavated finds, etc. but also in the instruments used in the performance of these processes[267] and in the descriptions given of the processes themselves. If related disciplines – drawing-centred or drawing-engaged – design, albeit not exclusively, through drawing practices, then the drawing instruments used in those practices, broadly and as I have argued above, must resemble one another. But archaeology also uses other kinds of tool which are not so readily mappable on to architectural equivalents. These are some which I have encountered whilst navigating from architecture towards archaeology: *trowels* are indirectly associated with architecture through their almost ubiquitous use on building sites, but as we will see[268] they are also used by archaeologists as drawing instruments; *sieves* are used to separate artefacts from their surrounding matrix where 'matrix' is defined as, "the material or sediment in which cultural debris is contained; the surrounding deposit in which archaeological finds are situated;"[269] A *Munsell Color Chart* is used to describe, in relation to objective standards, the colour of the matrix surrounding excavated artefacts; *radius charts* are sheets of, often, laminated paper printed with a series of concentric arcs of known radii on which to lay rim or base potsherd as a ready reckoner of the size of the original vessel; *profile gauges* are used in both architecture and archaeology (though less in architecture) to accurately measure small mouldings and other forms through their duplication. The gauge is usually a block through which pass a number of thin rods which, when pressed against a form, depress to retain the profile of that form.

Although this book argues that the tools and techniques of a discipline are inextricably linked with the practices and products of that discipline, there would seem to be few drawing-centred or drawing-engaged disciplines which have exclusive ownership over specific tools (even if, as I have argued above, the practitioners of some disciplines would like to claim such ownership) – I have not, for example, encountered any tools which are used by architects and architects alone.

The archaeological tools outlined above are used extensively in archaeological practice,[270] – especially field archaeology – but, with the exception of the radius chart, their use is not confined to it. However, taken as a sample of non-architecture-related tools they begin, I would argue, to outline an archaeology which has definitively diverged from architecture and, in particular, architecture's last common ancestor with archaeology; antiquarianism. They are tools which mediate between the hand of the archaeologist and the object of that archaeologist's attention; the trowel moves soil whilst the colour chart is placed directly against that soil – the potsherd is manually offered-up to the radius chart and the profile gauge is pushed against that potsherd or other artefact. From looking intently at artefacts, through touching and pushing them, to shifting the matrix which surrounds them, there is an immediacy about the wielding of these tools.

However, some tools do seem to be more specifically designed with a particular discipline in mind and these I have termed 'disciplinary tools.' They, especially in the examples analysed in this book, have been developed from within the discipline itself. With one exception it is this type of tool with which the rest of this chapter concerns itself, and even that exception is also recast, here, as a conceptual disciplinary tool.

The three conceptual disciplinary tools analysed below are all archaeological in origin since that is the transdisciplinary path navigated – from architecture towards archaeology – and argued here; the Chaîne Opératoire, the Decorative Frame and the Reflexive Seriation Diagram. This type of tool exists in architecture too; the R.I.B.A. Plan of Work with which the chaîne opératoire is compared is one, the architectural scale model – described by Albert Smith as, "a basic mechanism used to understand, explore and conceptualize architecture,"[271] and that "through the use of visual analogy and constructive metaphor, architectural models serve as measuring mechanisms extending the architect's intellectual might in an attempt to understand a complex and confusing whole"[272] – might be another. Neither is entirely exclusive to architecture but they are certainly meant for, or largely used by, architects and, like all conceptual disciplinary tools as I define them here, they tend to describe and manipulate processes rather than objects.

These tools operate instrumentally, in the philosophical sense; they make manifest otherwise nebulous approaches to disciplinary aims. For pragmatist philosopher William James, "this is the 'instrumental' view of truth [...] the view that truth in our ideas means their power to 'work.'"[273] For Dalibor Vesely architecture's instrumentality resides in its modern aim of achieving functional ends, abandoning its historical ability to carry meaning, "the transformation of architecture into an instrumental discipline with a formal purpose but with no explicit meaning, making it an instrument of pure ars inveniendi."[274] For him architecture, since the beginning of the eighteenth century, had become merely a tool for building shelter and for decorating it without reference to the history or tradition of those built forms and embellishments ensnared, as he saw them, in Jean-Nicolas-Louis Durand's "limited and naïve"[275] taxonomies of form.

Some tools, and in particular conceptual disciplinary tools, may reveal occluded disciplinary aims or offer alternative ways of apprehending otherwise conventional processes. These 'revelations' are precipitated through their interdisciplinary use or analysis. Three of these tools seem particularly fertile in this respect and my research into them advanced enough to outline here. The first manifests an archaeological process which describes the life cycle of lithic artefacts; the *chaîne opératoire* which has parallels in architecture with various schematisations of construction-centred building life-cycles, for example the R.I.B.A. Plan of Work. The second is a tool – and at first glance not a conceptual disciplinary tool – associated with excavation processes in archaeology; planning frames, or squares, are portable grids used to locate features for plotting and drawing. The third, seriation diagrams, are diagramming tools for organising the strata and artefacts of archaeological excavation.

1. The Chaîne Opératoire

I will only outline this tool since I have written about it in greater detail elsewhere.[276]

In the 1960s, with western narratives of technical progress at their height, Robert Matthew, then president of the Royal Institute of British Architects, and anthropologist André Leroi-Gourhan independently advocated totalising, systematic, technical models of human progress. Each model a reflection of the aims and methods of their own discipline: for the anthropologist, the evolution of *Homo sapiens* from *Homo faber* and the dissolving of human/technological boundaries; for the architect, a "collective welfare-socialism"[277] and the systematisation of its built manifestations. Each of these models were made manifest through profoundly influential diagrams. Leroi-Gourhan's *chaîne opératoire* describes the manufacture of prehistoric stone tools whilst the RIBA's Plan of Work describes the design and construction of buildings. Through the embodied objects and processes of these diagrams both "chaîne" and "Plan" engage in a kind of reciprocating exchange: a diagrammed conversation revealing, for each discipline, processes occluded or overlooked in the other.[278]

In particular, between the Plan of Work and the *chaîne opératoire,* common word use is identifiable and, where the language used is not identical, common concepts. More telling still are the differences between them; processes and concepts omitted or occluded. It is possible, for example, to see that the term 'Discard' is present and indeed crucial to the chaîne opératoire but absent in the

Plan – except as investment opportunities the place of the discarded, empty building is occluded in the kind of architectural practice represented by the R.I.B.A. Plan of Work. The Plan, in its most recent incarnation, refers to categories of, "In Use" and "post-occupancy," but these denote periods of occupancy post-handover of the completed building – not to periods of dereliction, decay and ruin. More centrally, this book has argued throughout that the notion of design is occluded in archaeology yet manifests itself in practices of reconstruction, and even a cursory examination of Plan and chaîne reveals that the 'design' categories in the architectural Plan are missing from, or occluded, in the archaeological chaîne.

2. The Decorative Frame

Accompanying the inexorable and increasing invisibility of London Stone itself there has been, amongst its occasional commentators, a persistent fascination with the artefacts which have, over the centuries, housed or framed or mediated it; etchings, paintings and photographs of it and its housing, its 'costume'. Textual references also describe these changes in costume. The following are typical;

> *1720*
>
> *The Stone before the Fire of London, was much worn away, and as it were but a Stump remaining. But is now for the Preservation of it cased over with a new Stone handsomely*

wrought, cut hollow underneath so as the old Stone may be seen, the new one being over it, to shelter and defend the venerable one.[279]

1869

London Stone Commonly believed to be a Roman Work Long placed about 35 foot hence Towards the South West And afterwards built into the Wall of this Church Was for more careful Protection And transmission to Future Ages Better secured by the Churchwardens In the Year of Our Lord 1869[280]

1901

a rounded block of stone of which a glimpse can be seen through the ornamental iron-work covering the stone receptacle – itself of great age – in which it rests.[281]

1958

the monument known as London Stone, now incorporated in the south wall of the church, shall be carefully removed and preserved by the Board and re-erected as near as possible to its present site.[282]

1964

During that century it was removed, set against the Church and later built into the Church wall, a protective grille being subsequently fixed for the stone's better protection.[283]

1972

'London Stone' with stone surround and iron grille set into base of number 111[284]

2006

It's in a kerbside cage, stuck on the wall of a sports shop in Cannon Street due for demolition.[285]

2015

housed in an aperture in the wall of number 111 Cannon Street (London EC4N 5AR), surrounded by a decorative Portland stone fascia with an iron grille. Inside the building it is protected by a glass case. The stone and its surround, with the iron grille, were designated a Grade II listed structure on 5 June 1972.*[286]

The decorative grille which fronted the Stone's niche is commonly believed to be the Victorian one depicted in Fig. 24. But upon close examination the metalwork is both cruder in detail and heavier in section. This subtle change and the addition of a glass screen behind the grille, probably both carried out in 1962, make the Stone when, as it often is, unlit, all but invisible. The decorative grid of the grille until recently dominated the Stone, making it difficult to see under normal lighting conditions. Indeed, any post-1869 representation of London Stone must therefore illustrate a view whose visual richness is overwhelming provided by everything but the Stone.

Obsessively drawing the Stone as an archaeological artefact, the grille in its domination of the Stone begins to organise and structure it just as an archaeologists' planning frame does. Viewed through the distorting 'lens' of this Decorative

Fig. 18 Alessandro Zambelli, London Stone sketched from a photograph. 2008, Digital photograph and CAD drawing.

Frame new and unlikely juxtapositions become possible as it explicitly alters the artefact beyond; accepting that it hides as much as it reveals (Fig. 18).[287] A planning frame is an excavation-recording tool and is used exclusively by archaeologists. The Concise Oxford Dictionary of Archaeology defines it as;

> *A square or rectangular chassis, typically 1m by 1m internally, that is used on archaeological sites to assist with accurately*

planning features, objects, or structures. [...] By laying the frame over an area that is to be planned or drawn, and locating the corners by offsets or triangulation, the planner can carefully observe the material to be drawn in relation to the grid within the planning frame and transfer this to scaled squares on the drawing board.[288]

By laying a planning frame over the object of their excavation, archaeologists are able to represent it with some accuracy and in relation to a datum. If, however, the faculty of reproducibility of the 10x10cm grid is substituted by some other, differently loaded medium, then the artefact is released from its subservience to a datum ordinarily required of an archaeological artefact and provided by the planning frame. At the same time the Stone and plinth are allowed to recede back into the building fabric of which they were once part (Fig. 19).

The history of London Stone is as much a history of that ever-reducing part of it made of oolitic limestoneas it is of the renewable contexts of building, street and grille. It is part of the mythos of London Stone that it resists the changes around it.The grille has at once arrested the erosion of the Stone and contributed to its invisibility. In *A propositional reconstruction* in the final chapter, the Stone is unhoused and, this time, both made visible and, then, allowed to literally disappear, witnessed by its intangible cast; Brutus, Los, Henry Fitz Ailwin, Jack Cade, Rebecca Daisy, Chris Cheek.

Fig. 19 Alessandro Zambelli, London Stone grille used as a planning frame. 2008, Photomontage. Original image: Robert Van de Noort/ Humber Wetlands Project. From: Kevin Greene, Archaeology: An Introduction, Fifth Edition, (London: Routledge, 2002).

3. The Reflexive Seriation Diagram

> *For many centuries it was popularly believed to be the stone of Brutus, brought by him as a deity. 'So long as the stone of Brutus is safe,' ran one city proverb, 'so long shall London flourish.'*[289]

Measuring only, "21 inches wide, 17 inches high and 12 inches front to back,"[290] other than this, almost everything else we think we know about London Stone has been demonstrated by its unofficial 'biographer,' John Clark, to be false or, as he puts it, "since it is so difficult to prove a negative, it is perhaps fairer to say that there is no evidence to support most of this farrago of myth."[291] These mythologies cleave to the Stone so readily precisely because of its unprepossessing physical presence – a mythology which grows in proportion to the extent that the Stone itself withers away; hidden by the erosions of time, the accrual of myth and the grilled housing which surrounds it. I propose that a conceptual disciplinary tool might be used to reveal occluded aspects of the Stone – unpacking the mythology surrounding it, re-connecting it back to the contemporary city and its cultures, folding back into itself its demonstrably 'fake' yet now vital traditions, folklore and legends. Moreover, I propose that the use of this tool might reclaim for the Stone a present, neither past nor future-facing. The Reflexive Seriation Diagram is a tool based upon archaeological seriation diagrams, but adapted and honed to examine layers of myth through the interrogation of 'representational strata' within which matrix the Stone sits, diagramming those layers as if they were archaeological strata. Elsewhere[292] I have proposed a common lineage between vernacular types of exploded drawing, and the archaeological seriation diagram, in particular the Harris Matrix. This particular association – this resemblance – makes the seriation diagram, I argued, available for interdisciplinary use.

Seriation diagrams, or seriation matrices, are tools used to stratigraphically organise features excavated on archaeological sites. Although ubiquitous they have been criticised for their tendency to narrow down the speculative possibilities of excavation, even to stand in for excavation itself;

> *The Harris matrix was originally intended to be an interpretative tool, and extensions of the basic idea were welcomed [...] Although some development work has taken place [...], there has been little critical analysis of the matrix, and its use has now become so universal that some archaeologists appear to have forgotten its original purpose. The stratigraphic matrix now is the archaeological site; it has ceased to be an aid to interpretation altogether, and has become a rather arcane representation of the entire process of excavation. Some archaeologists talk about the large size of their matrix as if this information alone is enough to suggest the richness and the complexity of the archaeology they have been encountering.*[293]

But as a tool that archaeologists, and not architects nor practitioners of any other discipline use, it lends itself as a tool for use in scandalous space. Figure 20 illustrates stills from a simple, animated, seriation diagram made to organise, in this case, representational material, both textual and image-based, concerning Raphael's Villa Madama – a building whose scandalous provenance is the

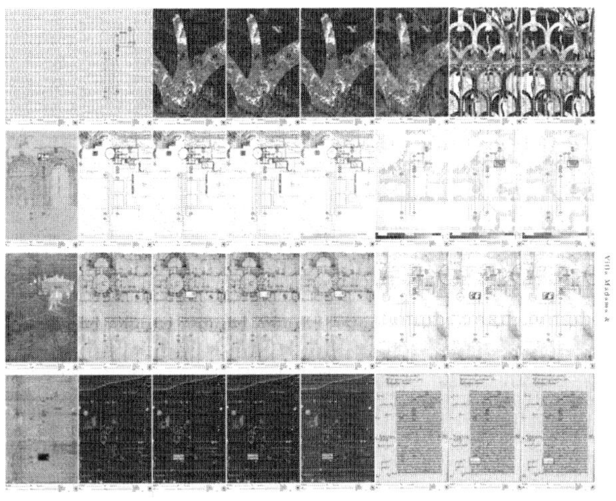

Fig. 20 Reflexive Seriation Diagram for Villa Madama. 2009, Edited sequence of stills from animation.

subject of investigation elsewhere,[294] and which I have used here for its intrinsic disciplinary looseness.

Villa Madama, in common with many historically significant buildings – buildings which have been around for long enough to have accrued a wealth of images of themselves – may be thought of as being composed of these temporal layers

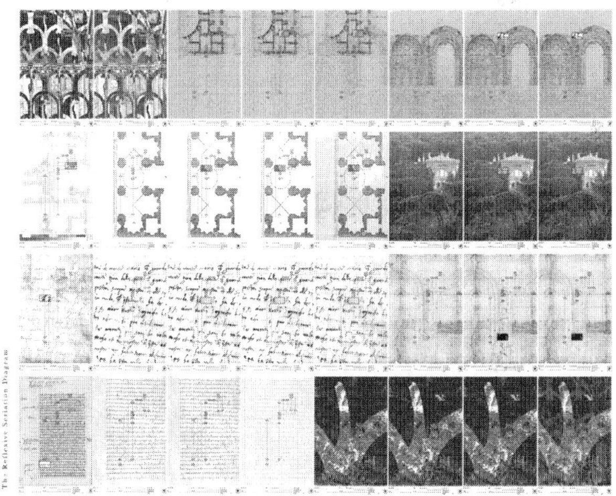

of representation. The Villa has, for example, gathered to itself variously: architectural precedent studies, sketches and layout options by its authors; photographs and sketches by historians and tourists; surveys and reconstructions also by architects and historians or, perhaps, by archaeologists. These representations will have been composed during the existing lifespan of the villa, and some influential representations (texts, for example, by Pliny the Younger upon which Raphael based his designs, and by Raphael himself to his client) which date from before the erection of the building fabric itself.

In this reflexive seriation diagram what would, in a standard Harris Matrix, have been archaeological strata are replaced with representational strata – these representations are key images of the villa from across its life-cycle, but includes also the production of new investigative drawings of it. All of the strata are then 'stacked' in chronological order. In a conventional Harris Matrix there is always an absolute top; undisturbed topsoil, say, and an absolute bottom; perhaps natural ground. These strata are schematised and their physical proximity recorded with interconnecting lines. In the modified seriation diagram there are no longer absolute limits to the matrix – it becomes circular, reflexive. It is reflexive because, for example, the very earliest representation of the Villa (in this case Pliny the Younger's early second century textual description of his Laurentine Villa)[295] is always in play either when Raphael uses it as a template for the design of his villa or when, much later, architects and architectural historians have attempted to reconstruct it. So, whereas conventionally the top-most and bottom-most strata are absolute and unconnected, when substituted for representational strata, proximity is no longer a matter simply of physical juxtaposition but of analogical relationship. From this 'raw' material I made the reflexive seriation diagram described above in the form of a brief, looped, film. This animated seriation diagram was designed to emphasise temporal movement down through the representational strata and to give some sense of the flow of information across the modified matrix rather than the conventional static or, at best, uni-directional bias of the Matrix. In preparation for the making of a new reflexive seriation diagram,[296] this time with London Stone as its object, a number of moves are made which combine the archaeologist's planning frame – the decorative frame described above – with the reflexive seriation diagram introduced here (Fig. 21). The frame is rendered as if it were a physical object placed over the subject of the representation and all within the principal picture plane. The wealth of mapping data available along with the presence of some, admittedly scarce, archaeological planning makes a plan-only series of representational strata possible. It also makes possible the use of the decorative frame as a "multi-informational" device to organise and record the mapping strata, so enabling their subsequent reconstruction in the concluding chapter of this book. These interdisciplinary appropriations and combinations are aimed at revealing the occluded architectural-archaeology and the archaeological-architecture of its object through strategies of visual analogy – in this case the visual mapping stratigraphy. Strategies made available by the felt-like medium of scandalous space to be outlined below.

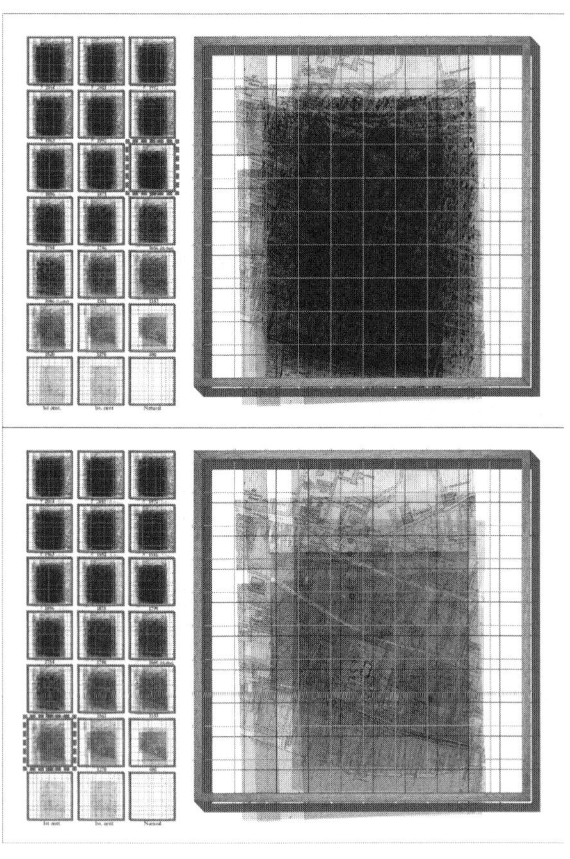

Fig. 21 Alessandro Zambelli, Archaeological strata as representational layers; every significant map centred upon London Stone, with superimposed Decorative Frame. 2015.

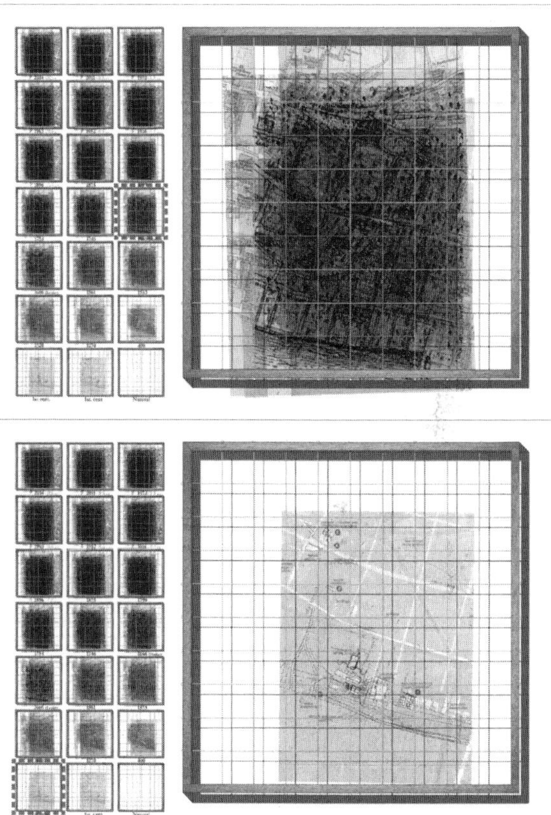

So, where the chronotopic aims to release the subject of its reconstruction from the linear tyranny of the chronological, the choreographic embraces the chronological but only in as far as time is counted as a 'partner' to its subject's 'dance' through it. This Instrumental Reconstruction works principally upon the contexts of its subject; its broader place in the "sequence of actions," its immediate physical contexts and its representational contexts. The next and final Chimaeric Reconstruction assembles all of these disparate fragments before their assembly in the concluding chapter.

Chimaeric Reconstruction

At the end of the Moves of London Stone guided tour the party were invited into a room within the Guildhall Library to discuss the tour and to look at some drawings produced in connection with the reconstruction of the Stone. One of those drawings was a 2.5m by 1.5m multi-part (500mm by 500mm squares) drawing incorporating some of the reconstruction investigations described above. An extract is illustrated in Figure 22.

The central element is a drawing describing a moment of mannered, stylised collision at the locus of the peripatetic movements of London Stone. The making of the drawing employs multiple instruments and techniques, some undisciplined, and the drawing itself implies some kind of reconstruction of London

Stone – presaging the propositional reconstruction drawing described below. At the frozen moment depicted, the drawing is in fact a dismantling of the Stone's site on and under Cannon Street. Sorrell's triumphal arch and the underground train whose floor coincides with Roman street level, are taken apart through techniques of exploded drawing which, as I have argued above, owe little to disciplined architectural or archaeological drawing practices, awaiting implosion and, finally, reconstruction. That is, waiting to be designed.

All of these reconstruction methods – Chronotopic, Choreographic, Instrumental, Chimaeric – describe practices aimed at alternative means of interrogating existing artefacts and proposing new ones. London Stone is already a scandalous artefact, but an accidental one. In dismantling and reconstructing it – re-designing it – the tools and techniques needed to practice in interdisciplinary, scandalous space are honed. The chimaeric drawing below (Fig. 22) is, therefore, a precursor to the 'propositional' reconstruction made in the next chapter; a sketch for it.

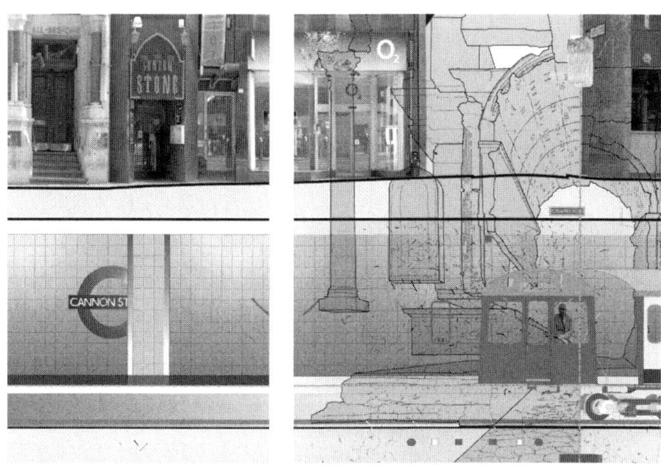

Fig.22 Alessandro Zambelli Chimaeric reconstruction of London Stone. [detail 1]. 2011-2018

Chapter 3

Chimaera

An Alternative Model for the Analogical Universe

If, for an archaeologist, to reconstruct an artefact, a building say, is to gather together fragments; client and user requirements, histories, contexts, finds, samples, assemblages etc., then the design practices of architects can also be understood as a form of reconstruction; a gathering together of fragments that is analogous to that in archaeological reconstruction. Once gathered, these fragments must be assembled, a process for which every design discipline has its own diverse sets of practices. In this book I have attempted to show that as common fragments are carried anaphorically back and forth between the knowledge systems of architecture and archaeology, they transform as they go; from Barbara Stafford's "magnified flea" to "silver goblet" to "fallen star" to "florentine stone." In this way I have attempted to navigate towards archaeology, carrying with me architectural tools, techniques and practices, transformed and revealed to be not so very different in either form or aim from those of archaeology.

In the scandalous space between architecture and archaeology, an *analogist* may practice by navigating between them – tacking to and fro – culminating, in this account, in speculatively produced (there is no particular, circumscribed, objective attached to its production), propositional, designs and reconstructions, which are simultaneously central to both disciplines and whose hybrid products are comprehensible. What, though, is to prevent those practices and their products becoming, instead, a disciplinary "hodgepodge" as Donald Campbell described it? – resembling, perhaps, Mary Shelley's tautological and tragic monster,[297] where the overlaying of (human) parts upon other (human) parts simply renders itself terminally self-referential, or perhaps the trivial, functional redundancy, of Hugh Lofting's Pushmi-pullyu.[298] In these accounts anything may be stitched together to hideous or trivial effect. Or, to use a different chimaeric model, in the Piltdown Man controversy archaeologist Charles Dawson attempted to design (because, in fact, there was no original skeleton to reconstruct) an early human, one that it was felt should have, but in fact never did, exist. A conceit resulting, like Homer's mythological Chimaera itself, in the production of a series of profoundly, temporally (and ethically) ambiguous, reconstructions.

So, in this concluding chapter, I will propose an alternative anaphoric cast to Stafford's flea, goblet, star and stone in order to more closely 'resemble' the "analogical universe." This analogical bestiary introduced above – Shelley's D.I.Y. 'monster,' and Lofting's double-headed, equivocating, antelope, set against Dawson's fraudulently assembled Hominin and Homer's mythical and monstrous, yet natural, hybrid – is preferred in this conclusion for their incipient and immanent agency. I will map each of them onto analogical categories provided by Mary Hesse and Dedre Gentner, and show whether, and how, each may be a medium of Latourian 'proposition' and 'offer.'

Hesse explains that analogical models are tools for expanding understanding of physical processes which proceed by "extending" such understanding as already exists as, she puts it, in "non-arbitrary" directions.[299] She invents the term, "neutral analogy" to distinguish this kind of reasoning from, "positive analogies" which are the tautological products of deductive logic and from, "negative analogies" which, for Hesse, produce only nonsense.[300] The neutral analogy owes to its key constituent part, the operation of abduction, the exploration and sometimes transgression of the boundaries of the traditional analogical model which had been derived from the biological sciences. Hesse emphasises the creative analogical reasoning intuited by Peirce;

> *theoretical concepts are to be understood as derived by analogy from situations familiar in observation and describable in observational terms. [...] analogy may give a basis for inductive analogical argument from systems that are known to exist and whose behaviour is known, so that by general induction, or what Newton called the 'analogy of nature', the behaviour of their less familiar analogues may be reasonably predicted.*[301]

Analogical reasoning becomes, as Peirce had

already guessed, a powerful tool for inferring the most likely, or best, explanation from uncertain data. As Hesse explains;

> *there will generally be some properties [...] about which we do not yet know whether they are positive or negative analogies, and these are the interesting properties, because, as I shall argue, they allow us to make new predictions.*[302]

Her theory of positive, negative and neutral analogies reveals a path from a pre-nineteenth-century realm of logical reasoning, via Peirce's discoveries regarding proto-creative reasoning, toward, I would argue, an analogical world of (logic-founded) resemblance and difference.

Gentner's analysis of different kinds of mappings in analogical mode, and the networks created by them,[303] embrace both physical attributes and attributes of appearance, that is, an analogy of the visual. Gentner has developed a way of categorising analogous or analogy-like relationships which builds upon Hesse's system of positive, negative and neutral analogies.[304] But now, through this analysis, rather than addressing single analogous relationships, we can think of suites of analogies forming sets of relationships. This web of relations begins to establish an environment the medium of which is analogy itself. Gentner's mapping clearly has its roots in Hesse's division of analogy types: her literal similarity is like Hesse's positive, tautological analogy; so many attributes are shared from base to target that no new association is likely to be drawn; the abstraction is a form of impoverished analogy – it functions analogically, yet reveals nothing. Her 'anomaly' is like a negative, nonsensical analogy, an association between base and target with such scarce resemblance between them, visual or otherwise that, according to Hesse and to Gentner, nothing novel could come of it. Yet I would not draw as a clear division between neutral and negative analogy as there is in Hesse's definition. Instead here, in this account, these analogical relationships are treated as extremes of one another – the extreme negative analogy producing nonsensical or trivial outcomes. In less extreme situations, scarce resemblance is strengthened through the juxtaposition itself and through the specific context of Gentner's analysis. So, though Gentner may be right in her terms to dismiss, "coffee is like the solar system," and as I shall argue below, Hesse warns against what she sees as this kind of trivial association where it may be possible that "relation exists between any two pairs of terms whatever,"[305] this type of correspondence is, nevertheless, an important one for the analogical universe. Its power is context-governed, that context being the principal analogical relationship of which the "anomaly" (again, in anything other than extreme manifestations) is an epiphenomenon and where the pre-figuring homology resides in the statement itself. In this account, this creative juxtaposition reignites the homological connection between sundered disciplines. In short the 'anomaly' is category of analogy where its terms share little or no resemblance. For meaningful interdisciplinary work (or scandalous practice) to be possible there must exist a homological proximity between the disciplines. If the disciplines drift too far apart, if their divergence becomes too profound, then the analogical relationship becomes anomalous in Gentner's terms or "negative" according to Mary Hesse.[306] It is only these extreme forms of the anomalous or negative analogy which preclude usefulness.

Both Shelley's "monster" and the Piltdown Man of, "amateur geologist, palaeontologist and archaeologist,"[307] Dawson concern the fabrication – the design – of scandalous (conventionally so at Piltdown) beings. Both have been successful creations in their own particular ways, due to the completeness of their respective gesamtkunstwerk; Shelley's monster embedded in late Georgian rationalism tinged with proto-Victorian romanticism, and Dawson's meticulously detailed promethean (though corrupt) inventiveness. As John McNabb explains, "it is vitally important to understand that the forger was not simply providing a faked ancestor, but was also giving it a material culture, animals with which to share its world, and aspects of that world's antecedents, as well as its descendants."[308] Although Dawson's interventions operated directly upon the practices of palaeontology and geology, Shelley's "monster," though removed from direct science practice is, poignantly, able to refer to itself in a way that Eoanthropus dawsoni has never been able to, "I ought to be thy Adam; but I am rather the fallen angel"[309] says the monster. In the terms of this book Frankenstein's "fallen angel" is positively analogical,[310] a tautological being, terminally self-referential; the "exaggerated singularity,"[311] as Stafford sees it, of allegory.

The creators of Piltdown Man were Dawson and his friend, geologist Arthur Smith Woodward;

> *The Piltdown forgery was an attempt to fabricate an ancient human ancestor, as well as the world that it came from. An important part of substantiating that world was to fabricate the material culture of* Eoanthropus dawsoni*, the Piltdown Man.*[312]

After Woodward and Dawson's formal presentation of their work to the Geological Society in December 1912 it was concluded that;

> *It was justifiable to associate the various fragments as parts of one human skull; and the simultaneous presence of so many simian characters in one and the same specimen was a point of great significance.*[313]

and that;

> *Although the skull and jaw pieces were awkwardly broken, Woodward reconstructed them into a complete skull that combined a modern-looking braincase with very ape-like jaws.*[314]

Woodward noted at the end of the presentation, perhaps echoing Frankenstein's contempt for his own creation, that "the swamps and forests of the Weald in early Pleistocene times may have been a refuge for a backward race."[315]

Lofting's fantastical invention, Doctor Dolittle's Pushmi-pullyu, like Shelley's "fallen angel," promotes a kind of operative and oppositional duplication.[316] It is a fatally compromised being; through its extreme symmetry every action is equally opposed by one performed by an exactly-duplicated self. The Pushmi-pullyu seems to directly reference the mythological Chimaera, another double-headed creature. Yet where the Chimaera's double nature is uncanny, that of the Pushmi-pullyu is dumbly reflective – each body can 'offer,' in the Latourian sense, nothing to the other.

Chimæra was the offspring of Typhon, "the largest monster ever born"[317] and Echidna an "irresistible" monster.[318] Homer described her as, "born of gods, not of men: she was a lion in front, a snake behind, and a goat in the middle, and her fearful breath was a blast of blazing fire."[319] A hybrid creature begotten of hybrid creatures, Chimaera was not stitched together but, like the Pushmi-pullyu, born to be that way. Unlike the Pushmi-pullyu, the Chimaera's hybrid parts work in concert with and not in opposition to one another. Tending towards the negatively analogical[320] (recall that this type of analogy, like Gentner's "anomaly" shares little resemblance between its terms) – resemblance is manufactured, as we have seen, through the juxtaposition itself. The scarceness of these kinds of chimaerical resemblance have troubled some commentators. Hesse voiced these concerns thus;

> *Any attempt to discuss the properties of an analogy-relation must begin by facing two opposite objections to the whole notion of analogy: the first on the ground that it is merely a trivial relation holding between certain pairs of terms, and the second on the ground that the relation exists between any two pairs of terms whatever, and is therefore useless*[321]

This is the most straightforward problem encountered when using analogy to generate meaning. Hesse answers her own first objection by elaborating on the nature of the, "pair of terms";

> *This, however, is hardly an adequate analysis of the analogy-concept as traditionally understood, for the assertion in the case of an analogy of a relation between a and b, and a relation between c and d, was always qualified by the remark that these two relations are not identical, but only similar in some relevant respect*[322]

Crucially she invokes the notion of "relevance" and in this account relevance is provided by the pre-figuring resemblance of a homological relationship.

The second objection is stronger; Hesse is aware for example that;

> *without further specification of S [where S is the relation between base and target terms] this does not help us with the present problem, because any possible method of correlating a with c and b with d would be a possible S, and thus, by choosing an appropriate S with a little ingenuity, any two pairs of terms could be shown to be related by analogy*[323]

This was Raymond Williams and Pierre Bourdieu's anxiety about homology being the thin end of an analogical wedge;[324] a potential free-for-all generating no meaningful relationships at all. Gentner's "coffee is like the solar system" – for her, an extreme nonsensical analogy –– is a case in point, dismissed by Gentner on exactly the grounds that Hesse sets out above. As Masaomi Kobayashi explains;

> *Bourdieu suspects that the homological method may become just an 'excuse for the vaguest kind of general formulations and the most unenlightening assertions of 'identity' between entities of utterly distinct magnitude and properties'*[325]

Of this second kind of objection, Hesse explains;

> *In classical discussions of analogy, this seems to have been provided by the ontology presupposed. For example, it might be assumed that both fields of relata of R and R' were independently ordered by a scala natura, making possible a 'proportion' between pairs of relata of R and corresponding relata of R''*

In other words Hesse appeals to Platonic proportional analogy, the "most beautiful bond possible;" a scala natura or chain of being.[326] The solution argued in this book is more straightforward. On the one hand it argues that coffee may in fact be like the solar system because, very simply, on this occasion Gentner has invoked it, and invoked it in a way which is, in this specific context, not trivial. She describes it in relation to what it is not; it is not any one of a number of other listed analogical types. On the other hand, it sits in the context of her work on *Structure Mapping*, in the Cognitive Science Journal, where she coins and defines the term such that in this specific context – though perhaps not others, "coffee is like the solar system" may obtain its wider and fully analogical meaning. That 'coffee' and 'the solar system' may have, or may be made to have, analogical connection is certainly not Gentner's intention – she uses it to demonstrate the opposite. Yet, I would argue that just as Chimaera's constituent lion, snake and goat parts function because of its Homeric and subsequent contexts, so can coffee be like the solar system.

Marxist literary critic Raymond Williams voices a final, different but related, kind of objection, when he says;

> *The most evident practical effect is an extreme selectivity. Only the cultural evidence which fits the homology is directly introduced. Other evidence is neglected, often with the*

explanation that the homologous is the significant evidence, and indeed is a way of distinguishing 'great works' from others.[327]

And this is precisely why the introduction of Gentner's anomalous or Hesse's negative analogy is important in this account; this kind of analogy actively seeks out new and strange relationships to "proposition" and from which to receive "offers" – the 'not fitting' (at least not quite) of lions, florentine stones, coffee, fleas, snakes, solar systems, chalices etc, is precisely the medium of Stafford's analogical universe. In the passage where Stafford introduces the notion of the analogical universe, she also sketches for us its general shape;

If the fragment, aphorism, ruin, grotesque and other shattered forms characterize allegorical compositions, then spinning, plaiting and weaving capture the simultaneity of contraries, the permeability and elasticity of intersubjective reciprocity. The analogical universe, like our membraned body, is knit together. It resembles a möbius strip, a continuous one-sided surface, investigated by topology, the mathematical study of geometric forms that do not change despite bending or stretching[328]

Stafford is attempting, here, to describe the analogical universe, but the array of metaphors she employs to describe it is contradictory. She variously uses "spinning," "plaiting," "weaving," but then reverts to a Deleuzian-sounding "membraned body" (which she then, paradoxically, notes is "knit" together). Her next move is to liken this analogical continuum to a möbius strip which is also Deleuzian, though the Lacanian reading is more pertinent here. Jacques Lacan uses the möbius strip to demonstrate the tendency for conventional psychoanalysis to reduce various binary distinctions, love/hate, inside/outside, to simple yet radical oppositions.[329] The möbius strip, of course, presents itself as an opposition but reveals itself to be continuous. Stafford refers to this potentially fertile ground only in passing, then returns to the fabric metaphor. What she fleetingly introduces, but which remains unacknowledged, is Gilles Deleuze and Felix Guattari's analysis of space where "fabric" and "felt" models are opposed to each other. Fabric, for them, is made of two kinds of parallel element set at right-angles to one-another (the warp and woof threads), one fixed, one mobile; fabric also has a top and a bottom. Fabric here, it seems to me, is like the mappings of analogy which, even when those mappings have multiple objects and targets, are constrained by the system of analogy itself. Both in their internal structure and in the orientation of space, fabric and the Gentner model of the analogical universe, are ultimately and profoundly limiting. Deleuzian felt-like space however, is described in this way;

[it] is a supple solid product that proceeds altogether differently, as an anti-fabric. It implies no separation of threads, no intertwining, only an entanglement of fibers

obtained by fulling (for example, by rolling the block of fibers back and forth). What becomes entangled are the microscales of the fibers. An aggregate of intrication of this kind is in no way homogeneous: it is nevertheless smooth, and contrasts point by point with the space of fabric (it is in principle infinite, open, and unlimited in every direction; it has neither top nor bottom nor center; it does not assign fixed and mobile elements but rather distributes a continuous variation).[330]

Here, Deleuze and Guattari offer a different but not unrelated account of Stafford's analogical universe to the logico-cognitive one outlined earlier. Ludwig Wittgenstein when outlining the phenomenon in language of "family resemblance" also adopted a felt-like model of resemblance for which the, "strength of the thread does not reside in the fact that some one fibre runs through its whole length, but in the overlapping of many fibres."[331] Deleuze and Guattari's description of hierarchical and non-hierarchical space shares structures of relationship with, as I have argued, the dependence of homology and analogy upon one another; their striated space of resemblance through proximity and interconnected origins, against smooth space defined instead by current, eddy and by other fluctuations in density.[332] For Stafford, as for Deleuze and Guattari, we are all, therefore, analogical agents inhabiting a space saturated by a kind of analogical aether or archaeological matrix; its complexity formed either from a kind of felt-like disorientation at the microscale or through changes in mass and consistency.

Deleuze and Guattari's felt-like smooth space may be read as a kind of precursor to Stafford's analogical universe inhabited, one imagines, by entities of pure analogy. Except that for Stafford, like Bourdieu, this universe is all hierarchy, where the analogical terms and the analogical continuum within which they exist are constructed entirely of Latour's "difference." All continuously "propositioning" one another, rejecting 'statements' of difference and embracing instead the interplay of difference and similarity, and providing the motive force for the transdisciplinary move between disciplines. This is Stafford's analogical universe properly underpinned by Alfred Gell's agency and index in propositional relationship to one another. For Gell, agency in the network of relationships in the world of art practice is abduction-based, just as it is across the network of relationships in scandalous space. This logical operation of abduction, which is described by Latour as an "offer," provides an armature for the wunderkammer that is lacking in Stafford's own account of visual analogy.

A Propositional Reconstruction

The reconstructions outlined in the previous chapter, and in this reconstruction, are neither conventionally architectural, though that is my base discipline, nor are they recognisably archaeological, though it is that discipline towards which I have navigated. As these reconstructions have developed they have exhibited signs of their shared lineage in both parent disciplines. They use archaeological knowledge, tools, techniques and practices acquired at the 'sites of encounter' described here and adapted through interaction with architectural knowledge, tools, techniques and practices. This work occurs in scandalous space, revealing and using the reconstructive practices of architecture and the design practices of archaeology. They are simultaneously sketches for this final, speculative propositional reconstruction of London Stone and they are themselves part of that final reconstruction.

Recent designs for the re-housing of the Stone have attempted to revive its lost visibility. Figure 23 shows the recently re-housed Stone. A 2011 scheme which proposed moving the Stone approximately forty meters to the west was met with widespread opposition. This, from the Victorian Society to the Corporation of London planning department, is typical;

> *the precise location of London Stone is highly significant – while it has crossed Cannon Street it seems to have been placed opposite St Swithin's for the entire recorded history of London. The symbolism of moving it from this place because the owners of the building find its presence inconvenient is appalling.*[333]

Fig. 23 London Stone in its most recent housing at 111 Cannon Street.

Both of these proposals (as well as variations of each which have been submitted to the local authority for planning approval) start from the assumption that the venerability of the object makes it a museum-piece available to current mainstream curatorial practice – what has been described as, "the new orthodoxy of visitor sovereignty;"[334] the artefact must be made more accessible, more visible, and aids provided for its interpretation. An approach the Victorian Society opposes in another letter objecting, this time, to a more recent proposal;

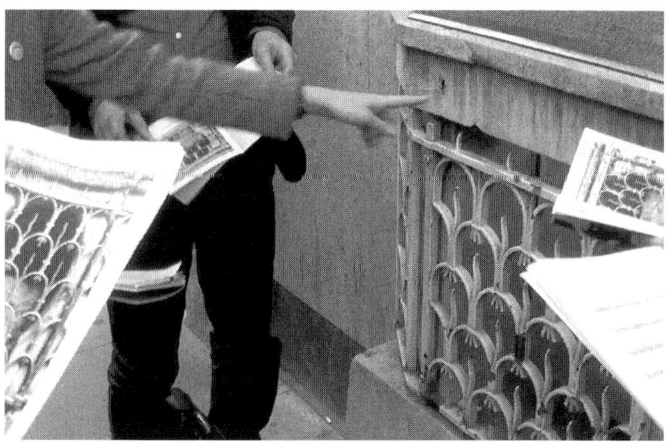

Fig. 24 Eleanor Suess, The Moves of London Stone tour: Emma Cheatle spots the difference between new and old grilles [still from footage]. 2013, Digital film.

The Victorian grille behind which the Stone is currently kept allows a partial view of it, which is eminently suited to its history and the nature of its significance, and adds to its air of mystery. The application proposes to make the Stone more of a museum-piece, by placing it in an illuminated glazed box. This approach is misconceived. It is not an object of beauty and craftsmanship which is designed to be admired and requires careful scrutiny; displaying it in this way would strip it of its enigmatic qualities.[335]

Unfortunately they also refer to its, "appropriate and long-standing Victorian grille," describing it as a "significant element of its importance and should be preserved."[336] Comparison of photographs from 1869 and 2013 demonstrate that the grille is more likely to be a twentieth-century replacement (Fig. 24).[337]

I conclude this chapter and this book with one final reconstruction. It is speculative, and it is propositional in the sense derived from Latour, that is; it is based upon an indexical relationship between maker and artefact, and characterised, after Peirce, by the creative suggestion that "something may be."[338] Figure 25 describes a drawing I made (and continue to make) during the navigations made available by these terms and associated concepts. They are designs, and they are simultaneously propositional reconstructions of the artefact of which London Stone was, and will be, part.

In this drawing, London Stone is read as an image and a text amongst other images and texts, both physically adjacent and temporally distant, their connection being one of resemblance. In particular, present in this propositional reconstruction, the figures of Jack Cade and Rebecca Daisy, introduced at the beginning of this book and again in Choreographic Reconstruction, are re-united with the Stone. Alongside them is arrayed a host of other interlocutors, each of whom has appeared in a drawing, etching, painting or photograph of the Stone. Some also featured in the stories I told about the Stone during *The Moves of London Stone* tour. In this propositional reconstruction they re-appear, resembling one-another in their common reliance upon the mythologising Stone. London Stone is reconstructed from this matrix, or felt-like substrate, of resemblances.

This drawing is an on-going work and begins to employ some of the undisciplinary drawing techniques outlined above – Rebecca's new "sweetstuff" stall is exploded (Jack, perhaps a little over-enthusiastically – yet protectively I like to think – waves his sword), otherwise, everyone chats convivially in this mise-en-scène. Jonathan Hill and Chris Cheek stand upon a multi-informational plan of the street beneath them. Indeed, the entire drawing is a multi-informational image and, perhaps, a site of encounter in its own right too.

London Stone itself is returned to its likely original

location, once again a menace to traffic. A vertical shaft beneath it re-connects it to Roman street level, a cut through the road and pavement points to its previous locations against the buildings that have occupied 111 Cannon Street. The Stone is unprotected; its eventual erosion, and complete disappearance, hastened—any further need for its physical presence satisfied.

The interdisciplinary work of the London Stone reconstructions is enabled by the transdisciplinary movement – tacking – at the sites of encounter described above and below. Despite architecture's tendency to dominate the other, its "weakness" as a discipline, its permeability to other disciplines,[339] as well as its homological proximity to archaeology, enables the making of these kinds of reconstructive drawing. Even so, the transdisciplinary 'move' is an adventure, and so speculative, and although made, as I have argued and experienced, through "immobile," "intensive," "speed," it is a journey to be taken in humility. The enormity of the discipline towards which the analogist navigates, however welcoming, appears from a distance sublimely vertiginous, and demands this humility. The interdisciplinary practice which attends these transdisciplinary movements are, as Latour's terminology of magnanimity – proposition and offer – suggests, reciprocal acts of generosity between disciplines, and this has certainly been my experience. Archaeology makes available to architecture its evidence-based practices of excavation, assemblage, find, including as we have seen an understanding of, "taphonomic forces, accumulation, sedimentation, reuse, repeated activity, truncation, chaîne d'opératoire"[340] as well as a range of technical, in-situ, drawing practices. In response, architecture reveals for archaeology types of speculative engagement with that evidence.

Fig. 25 [opposite] Alessandro Zambelli, The Return of Jack and Rebecca: a propositional reconstruction. 2018, Mixed media.

The Return of Jack and Becky

Site of Encounter

Must Farm

Must Farm near Whittlesey in Cambridgeshire is a significant archaeological site encompassing features from the Mesolithic to the late bronze age. It has featured in a number of popular radio and television broadcasts and in 2012 it won Best Project and Best Archaeological Discovery at the British Archaeological Awards. Senior Project Officer Mark Knight explains that;

> Must Farm is changing the way Fenland archaeology is viewed. Once regarded as a barren landscape with little to offer, the emergence of deep space archaeology is revealing artefacts that are surprising in both their quantity and quality.[341]

On the outskirts of Peterborough, one hundred and fifty years ago, pits up to thirty metres deep were dug in order to access the Lower Oxford Clay required for the ever-popular London Stock Bricks. Coincidentally, and fortunately for the nascent disciplines of palaeontology, and subsequently archaeology, these great depths enabled local farmer and proto-palaeontologist Alfred Nicholson Leeds to extract dinosaur bones from deep, completely undisturbed, strata using relatively non-destructive methods, "the brick-pits made access to the deepest sediments feasible" explains Knight, "and, at the same time, the early methods of extraction prior to mechanisation were conducive to locating 'anomalies' in the clay."[342]

The brick pits are still in use and collaboration between Hanson P.L.C. who, under their parent company Heidelberg Cement Group, run the quarry, and the Cambridge Archaeological Unit – the archaeologists digging just ahead of the advancing mechanical excavators – means that large swathes of buried Neolithic and bronze age inhabited landscapes are available to detailed archaeological investigation;

> In the fens, time covers space: it does not efface or rub

away past occupations — instead it buries things deep. Fenland is a landscape that has tremendous depth as well as great breadth.[343]

Deep space archaeology is different because it is invisible from the surface, its very depth making it impervious to disturbance, both now and in the past.[344]

In the summer of 2012 I was invited by Lesley McFadyen of Birkbeck's Department of History, Classics and Archaeology to participate in their Fieldschool module at Must Farm. In the three days of participation my aims were twofold: firstly to understand, as far as it is possible to understand from such a brief and partial encounter, something of the nature of how archaeologists excavate – to see how those excavations are directed and to take part in the digging itself; and secondly to participate in the drawn recording of artefacts if the opportunity presented itself.

The excavations were run on a day to day basis by Cambridge Archaeological Unit; Knight and two colleagues Lizzy Middleton and Leane Zeki. Birkbeck Fieldschool Director McFadyen was in charge of the students.

For the occasion I had bought, amongst other things, a foam kneeling pad and a 4" W.H.S. trowel. Trowels have an almost mythical status amongst field archaeologists who can become very attached to particular ones,[345] much as architects used to become attached to particular drawing pens or set-squares;

Some live for the flexibility of a Marshalltown and some enjoy the style personified in a French trowel. We say nothing is more elegant than a sturdy W.H.S.[346]

Field archaeologists often draw with their trowels,[347] and of course, trowels are also a builder's tool (recall Tim Ingold's elision of architect and builder through the trowel above p.8) – a tool for making; allying the archaeologist even more closely, perhaps, to the making of buildings than the abstracted distance of the architect. The trowel and the foam kneeling-pad reminded me that field archaeology is a much more physical discipline than architecture – site visits for architects often involving no more than the ability to climb scaffold ladders and, on larger building sites, there are usually lifts providing access to most parts of the works.

The following are lightly edited excerpts from my site diary:

Must Farm, Whittlesey

16th July *occasional light rain*

9.30 – 4.00

After a thorough introduction to the site by Mark, its history and topography, each student was given a 1m square of ground to excavate.

I was shown, by example, how to scrape away layers of the earth, identifying possible artefacts as I went and placing them in a finds tray, until I encountered what had already been identified elsewhere as the level of natural (darker) soil.

Throughout the entire depth of my test pit (and most others) were the mineralised remains of worm casts and reed cases.

My square was adjacent to an already excavated area identified by Lesley as the location of a middle-Neolithic area of 'tree throw'. That is, a tree had fallen over 'throwing up' soil from underground over what would have been the existing topsoil at the time, so locally inverting the expected order of soil deposit. That this unexpectedly darker soil formed an arc was indicative of a tree throw.

Lesley explained the process of and the evidence for the tree throw on a number of occasions, at one point demonstrating through drawing with her trowel directly into the soil to highlight features.

From time to time Mark or Lesley would go through the contents of each student's finds tray identifying which objects were 'real' and so artefactual and those which were not and therefore natural, and to be discarded.

During the course of the day I found some small pieces of worked flint.

17th July overcast then sunny

9.30 – 4.00

In the morning I continued with the excavation of my test pit, finding some more pieces of worked flint.

After lunch I was offered the chance to survey and draw an artefact on the other side of the site exposed earlier in the week by a Birkbeck student. The survey was directed by Cambridge Archaeological Unit archaeologist Lizzy Middleton.

The artefact was an approximately 800mm long twisted piece of timber crudely worked to a rough point at one end. It had been dated stratigraphically to the Middle-Neolithic and was part of a series of features, including evidence of a line of thinner fence-posts and a 'monument', all found in the immediate vicinity (Fig. 26). The 'stake' was still in situ when it was surveyed and was periodically sprayed with water to delay its deterioration.

Lizzy fixed a line with a peg into the vertical face of an adjacent test pit, ran it across the front of the stake and fixed its other in a similar fashion. A datum was fixed on the line and a little to the left of the stake. Lizzy read off dimensions above and below the line, at fixed distances along it, to significant features of the stake which I plotted, first simply as dots, on to the sheet of Permatrace waterproof graph paper.

Once the outline of the stake had been filled in, along with its more significant structural elements, we discussed what kinds of additional features should be shown and possible graphic techniques for the illustration of those features. Three principal features were identified and graphic techniques adopted for each of them: worked faces; charring; sand encrustation. In each case I decided what the graphic convention would be, Lizzy advising as to any conflicts with standard archaeological conventions. In particular the dotted hatching I used for the sand is often used to indicate stone artefacts, but because of the context, the likeness of the hatch to the sand itself but principally because of the inclusion of a key to graphic techniques, we agreed that it would work and could stand.

As we were completing the survey Mark came to look at the drawing and the stake. The intense scrutiny required in making a survey meant that the parts of the stake which Lizzy identified as being charred were more obvious than they had previously been. In addition whilst drawing the stake its surface had become quite dry making the darker patches more prominent still. Mark, viewing the stake when it had once again been moistened, was less certain that the dark patches were evidence of burning than Lizzy had been.

Once the survey had been completed I returned to my test pit and carried on excavating it for the rest of the day.

Fig. 26 [opposite] Alessandro Zambelli, Partially excavated stake. 2012, Digital photograph and measured drawing of bronze age stake. 2012, Photocopy, pencil on Permatrace. Measurements [and much advice]: Lizzy Middleton, Cambridge Archaeological Unit.

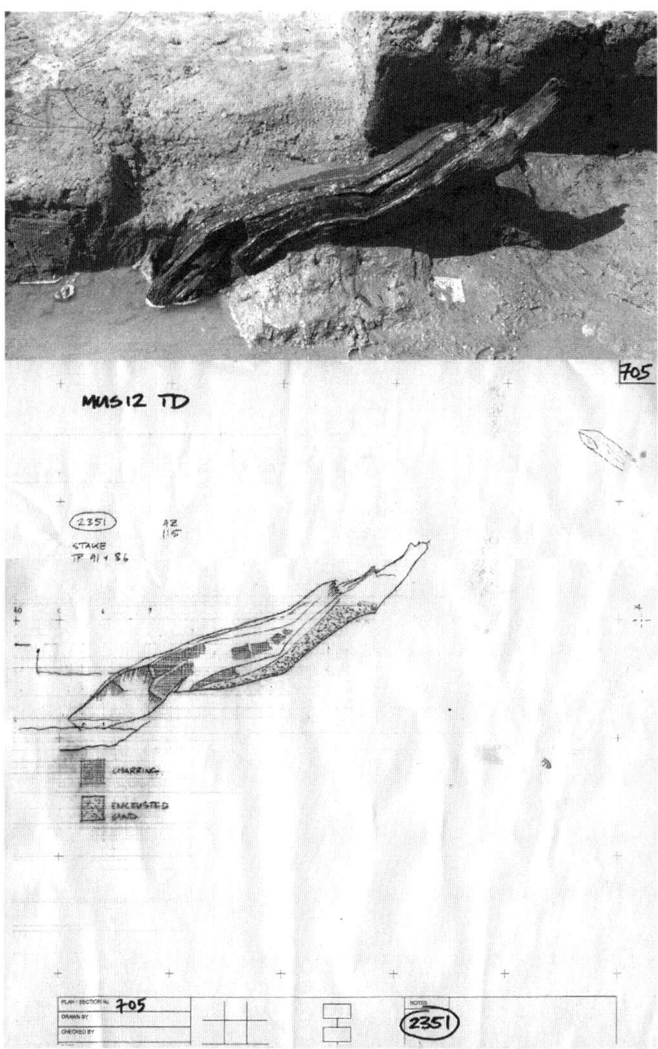

705
MUS12 TD
2351
AZ
115
STAKE
TP 91 + 86
CHARRING
ENCRUSTED SAND
PLAN / SECTION No 705
DRAWN BY
CHECKED BY
NOTES
2351

18th July cloudy but dry – later heavy rain becoming thundery – excavation abandoned because of electrical storm

9.30 until abandoned

In order to clear the group of test pits amongst which I was working the team in that area sped up. In particular I started taking less care than I had previously in identifying potential artefacts. In retrospect I think there was a general feeling that the group of pits, with the exception of a pit at the opposite end of our group which yielded a post (which subsequently proved to be part of a line of posts),[348] *had given up all they were going to.*

As Mark Knight developed excavation strategy on the spot, reacting to the things found and not found, so I witnessed the archaeological production of culture and histories through discursive processes. Deciding whether such and such piece of wood was an artefact, what kind of artefact it was, what processes and practices were evidenced by it, whether it had been burned or not, were all small but potentially significant creative moves as, I would argue, cultures and artefacts were being designed.

Two modes at least of drawing were used; one as a pedagogical tool – a WHS 4" trowel employed to inscribe into the medium of the soil itself and the more straightforward recording of an extant artefact by pencil on paper. In both cases the drawing tools were used as part of a design process which included discursive elements – marks would be made, perhaps revised, discussed and knowledge produced.

In both Institute of Archaeology classes I had taken in 2010[349] *and the Must Farm excavation of 2012 my presence and role were difficult to classify. In particular the status of my drawing of the stake – now in the archaeological archive of the project along with drawings made by archaeologists – is a curious one. After the event I asked Lizzy Middleton what kind of drawing she thought I had produced; did she even think of it as an archaeological drawing? She replied;*

I often think about the way you represented the stake and the different styles in which [...] we showed the 'burning' and facets and features upon the wood.[350]

Firstly I would say that your drawing is definitely an accurate 'field drawing', maybe with a little architectural flare!

So I would say your stake is a very accurate 'field drawing', it definitely fits into this bracket, with the main criteria for such being

- conveying the archaeology honestly

- showing the archaeology cleanly and clearly, almost keeping it quite simplified.[351]

I had also asked Lizzy about the immediacy of archaeological field drawings compared with the kinds of drawings which architects might make. In her reply she emphasised this speed and immediacy;

I think on the whole, archaeologists seem to think that when on site its important to get all the information down on the plan and then when it goes back to the office, to the graphics department, that's where it will be digitised and made 'pretty.' However I think a lot of us feel that when on site you're seeing the artifact at its best, it's freshly exposed and it will never look as good again, [...] the objects will inevitably deteriorate and with wood in particular, chop marks or features upon it may be lost over this time period. I think that's why on the whole we try to draw it straight away as well as we can, using the conventions.[352]

She admitted that there were exceptions to the absolute priority given to speed;

On site the priority is to get the information down accurately and clearly - if you make it aesthetically pleasing then this is a bonus in a way. With Must Farm the sort of drawing opportunities we encounter are a bit of an exception and it certainly isn't the usual type of recording (being waterlogged wood). Therefore it has given us the opportunity to exercise different techniques and enabled the show of artistic skill. Another example would be when planning skeletons – this too would be a rarer occurrence to the everyday recording.[353]

Clearly Must Farm is an exceptional site as evidenced by the awards it subsequently won.

Recalling a conversation I had had with archaeologist Dominic Perring some years earlier when he had expressed surprise at my characterisation of the single context plans he was showing me as 'austerely beautiful,' I pressed Lizzy on the issue of drawing quality asking, perhaps naively;

When architects draw, even technical drawings, there is always a compulsion to make them as beautiful as they can be – that may simply mean drawing as clearly and simply as possible. I'm not sure that archaeologists, by and large, think of their drawings in this way.[354]

And got the reply I deserved;

I think, personally, I do take great pride in how I draw and represent whatever I'm recording on site, whether it be a wooden artifact or feature or a section of a pit. However some things would make me want to spend more time on, depending on its importance. For example the Must Farm boats I would spend quite a while getting just right, where as a stake I would just do as quickly as possible. Having said that I would still want it to look good![355]

My brief participation in the Must Farm Excavation had been long in the planning – I needed an excavation where I was not simply volunteer labour and which was also run as a training dig but at a somewhat more advanced level than other kinds of common training event. McFadyen wrote of it;

Birkbeck students are older than those from other universities, and many of them do want to become practising archaeologists, so I have designed the field school so that it gives them a bit more of a head start over other students (it is not just training, it is work experience).[356]

Must Farm has not been the last 'tack' in my transdisciplinary journey towards something like archaeology, from something like architecture. Papers delivered at Theoretical Archaeology Group conferences at Chicago[357] and at Bournemouth are also 'tacks' in this account (see Fig. 1). Yet Must Farm was significant for its connections, not just with academia, but also with commercial archaeology. It was also significant for me, for the lodging of my drawing – a drawing by an architect – in the project archive (Fig. 26).

Architects are regular contributors to large archaeological projects, but their work is the multidisciplinary product of their typical role as consultant or interpreter, and is rarely viewed as archaeology. For example, even on a project which spreads its disciplinary net as far as that at Çatalhöyük, no architect has been involved in recent years.[358]

Together, the tacks made at these particular sites of encounter define a space for interdisciplinary practice both between and within (the disciplines of archaeology and architecture), within because the influence of disciplinary ripples recede infinitely from strong professionalised centres. In Fig. 1 this space is labelled 'London Stone Reconstructed.'

If the diagram of the architect tacking towards archaeology (Fig. 1) is reproduced, 'zoomed out' as it were (Fig. 28) then we gain a different perspective of these truly adjacent disciplines, revealed to be only slightly out of phase with one another in an ocean of disciplinary ripples. If this oceanic, analogical, medium resembles Deleuze and Guattari's "supple solid"[359] *felt, then perhaps 'navigation,' per se, is rendered unnecessary and the chart of the scandalous space between architecture and archaeology becomes obsolete, "the freeing of a line that does not pass between two points."*[360] *The architect making the transdisciplinary move to practice towards archaeology is still an architect even when sitting in a muddy test pit, pencil in hand.*

In Figure 27 that architect and an archaeologist sit drawing together. The architect already knows how to draw, but here and now, at this site of encounter, he knows only architecture; archaeology an enticing and scandalous intimation. Meanwhile, the archaeologist, carefully, teaches him to draw again.

Fig. 27 Lesley McFadyen, Alessandro Zambelli with Lizzy Middleton at Must Farm. 2012, Digital photograph.

Fig. 28 [overleaf] Alessandro Zambelli, Spatial diagram of disciplines. Homological relationship creates a "proximity." 2014.

Bibliography

Ackroyd, Peter. London: *The Biography*. London: Vintage, 2001.

Alexander, Christopher. *Notes on the Synthesis of Form*. Cambridge, Mass.: Harvard University Press, 1964.

Allen, Thomas, and Thomas Wright. *The History and Antiquities of London, Westminster, Southwark and Parts Adjacent.* With Engravings. 5 vols. Vol. 3, London: G. Virtue, 1827.

Alÿs, Francis. "Seven Walks." Artangel, http://www.artangel.org.uk/projects/2005/seven_walks.

Anderson, Jane. *Basics Architecture 03: Architectural Design*. Lausanne ; Worthing: AVA Academia, 2011.

Anon. *The British Apollo, or, Curious Amusements for the Ingenious. To Which Are Added the Most Material Occurrences Foreign and Domestic. Perform'd by a Society of Gentlemen*. [with Indexes to Vol. 1 3.] Vol. 1. No. 1-Vol. 4. No. 20. 13 Feb. 1708-11 May, 1711. London: J. Mayo, for the Authors, 1708.

———. "The Cannon Street Stall-Keeper." *The Daily Graphic*, 24 April 1901.

———. "London Stone." *Chambers's Journal* 5th Series (21st April 1888).

———. "London Stone." Wikipedia, https://en.wikipedia.org/wiki/London_Stone.

Archaeology, Society for American. "What Is Archaeology?" *Society for American Archaeology*, http://www.saa.org/publicftp/public/educators/03_whatis.html.

An Architect, "Letter." *The Gentleman's magazine* 68 Part 2, no. 3 (1798): 735-822.

Bahn, Paul G. *The Penguin Archaeology Guide*. Rev., expanded and updated ed. London: Penguin, 2001.

Bakhtin, M. M. *The Dialogic Imagination: Four Essays*. Translated by Caryl Emerson. edited by M. Holquist Austin: University of Texas Press, 1981.

Baranski, M.Z. "Back to Mellaart a Area: Survey on Late Neolithic Architecture." *Çatalhöyük 2013 Archive Report* (2013): 220-34.

Barry, Andrew, and Georgina Born. "Interdisciplinarity: Reconfigurations of the Social and Natural Sciences." In *Interdisciplinarity: Reconfigurations of the Social and Natural Sciences*, edited by Andrew Barry and Georgina Born, 1-56. London; New York, NY: Routledge, 2013.

Bean, Jonathan, and Daniela Rosner. "Old Hat: Craft Versus Design?". *ACM Interactions January-February* (2012): 86-88.

Benjamin, Walter. *The Arcades Project*. Translated by Howard Eiland and Kevin McLaughlin. Cambridge, Mass. ; London: Belknap Press, 1999.

Blake, William. Milton. *A Poem*, Etc. [with Illustrations by W. Blake.]. pl. 45. W. Blake: [London,] 1804 [1808?]. 1804.

Blau, Eve, Edward Kaufman, and Robin Evans. *Architecture and Its Image: Four Centuries of Architectural Representation*. Montreal:

Centre Canadien d'Architecture, 1989.

Borges, Jorge Luis. "Tlön, Uqbar, Orbis Tertius." Translated by Donald Alfred Yates and James E. Irby. In *Labyrinths: Selected Stories and Other Writings*. Harmondsworth: Penguin, 1970.

Bourdieu, Pierre. *Outline of a Theory of Practice*. Translated by Richard Nice. Cambridge: Cambridge University Press, 1977.

Bourdieu, Pierre, and Jean-Claude Passeron. *Reproduction in Education, Society and Culture* [in Translation of: La reproduction.]. Translated by Richard Nice. London: Sage, 1990.

Bremner, Craig, and Paul Rodgers. "Design without Discipline." *Design Issues* 29, no. 3 (2013/07/01 2013): 4-13.

Brennan, Tim. "The Manoeuvre." *Visual Studies* 25, no. 1 (2010/03/23 2010): 80-81.

Brunskill, R. W. *Vernacular Architecture: An Illustrated Handbook*. 4th ed. London: Faber, 2000.

Burton, Anthony. "Design History and the History of Toys: Defining a Discipline for the Bethnal Green Museum of Childhood." *Journal of Design History* 10, no. 1 (1997): 1-21.

Burton, Gail, Serena Korda, and Clare Qualmann. "Walkwalkwalk: An Archaeology of the Familiar and the Forgotten." http://www.walkwalkwalk.org.uk/.

Butler, Ann B., and William Hodos. *Comparative Vertebrate Neuroanatomy: Evolution and Adaptation*. 2nd ed. Hoboken, N.J.: Wiley-Liss, 2005.

Camden, William, and Philemon Holland. *Britain, or, a Chorographicall*

Description of the Most Flourishing Kingdomes, England, Scotland, and Ireland ... Written First in Latine by W. Camden ... Translated Newly into English by Philemon Holland ... Finally Revised, Amended, and Enlarged with Sundry Additions, Etc. Londini, 1610.

Campbell, Donald T. "Ethnocentrism of Disciplines and the Fish-Scale Model of Omniscience." In *Interdisciplinary Relationships in the Social Sciences*, edited by Muzafer Sherif and Carolyn W. Sherif, xvi, 360 p. Somerset, N.J.: AldineTransaction ; London : Eurospan [distributor], 2009.

Cardiff, Janet. "The Missing Voice: Case Study B." http://www.cardiffmiller.com/artworks/walks/missing_voice.html.

Carpo, Mario. *The Alphabet and the Algorithm*. Cambridge, Mass. ; London: MIT Press, 2011.

———, ed. *The Digital Turn in Architecture 1992 2012*. Chichester: Wiley, 2012.

Carr, Edward Hallett. *What Is History?: The George Macaulay Trevelyan Lectures Delivered in the University of Cambridge January-March 1961*. Harmondsworth: Penguin, 1987.

Cassanelli, Roberto, and Massimiliano David. *Ruins of Ancient Rome: The Drawings of French Architects Who Won the Prix De Rome, 1786-1924* [in Translated from the Italian.]. Los Angeles: J.P. Getty Museum, 2002.

Chadwick, Adrian. "Archaeology at the Edge of Chaos: Further Towards Reflexive Excavation Methodologies." *Assemblage,* no. 3 (January 1998).

Clark, John. "Jack Cade at London Stone." *Transactions of the London*

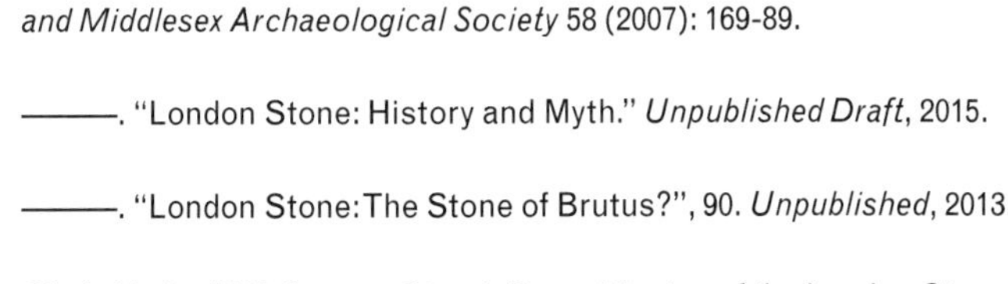
and Middlesex Archaeological Society 58 (2007): 169-89.

———. "London Stone: History and Myth." *Unpublished Draft*, 2015.

———. "London Stone:The Stone of Brutus?", 90. *Unpublished*, 2013.

Clark, Kathy. "111 Cannon Street, Repositioning of the London Stone (Grade 2*, Origins Unknown, 19th Century Grille and Plaque)." 2: *The Victorian Society*, 2013.

Coles, Alex, and Alexia Defert. *De-, Dis-, Ex-. Vol.2, Anxiety of Interdisciplinarity*. London: BACKless Books in association with Black Dog Publishing, 1998.

———. "Introduction." In *De-, Dis-, Ex-. Vol.2, Anxiety of Interdisciplinarity*, edited by Alex Coles and Alexia Defert, pp.i-iii. London: BACKless Books in association with Black Dog Publishing, 1998.

Costelloe, Chris. "Re: Relocation of London Stone (Grade Ii*, Uncertain Date, C19 Iron Grille) from 111 Cannon Street to the Walbrook Building." 2: *The Victorian Society*, 2011.

"Cotúa Island-Orinoco Reflexive Archaeology Project." UCL Institute of Archaeology, http://www.ucl.ac.uk/archaeology/research/directory/orinoco-reflexive-oliver.

Coughlan, Sean. "London's Heart of Stone." BBC, http://news.bbc.co.uk/1/hi/magazine/4997470.stm.

Cousins, Mark. "Building an Architect." In *Occupying Architecture: Between the Architect and the User*, edited by Jonathan Hill. London: Routledge, 1998.

Cross, Nigel. *Designerly Ways of Knowing*. London: Springer, 2006.

Crow, Michael M., and William B. Dabars. *Designing the New American University*. Baltimore: Johns Hopkins University Press, 2015.

Crowne, John. "The Misery of Civil War [1681]." In *Shakespeare Adaptations from the Restoration : Five Plays*, edited by Barbara A. Murray. Madison [N.J.]: Fairleigh Dickinson University Press, 2005.

Darvill, Timothy. *The Concise Oxford Dictionary of Archaeology*. 2nd ed. New York: Oxford University Press, 2008.

Darwin, Francis, ed. *The Foundations of the Origin of Species: Two Essays Written in 1842 and 1844 by C. Darwin*. Cambridge: University Press, 1909.

Dawson, C, and A. S. Woodward. "On the Discovery of a Palaeolithic Human Skull and Mandible in a Flint-Bearing Gravel Overlying the Wealden (Hastings Beds) at Piltdown, Fletching (Sussex)." *Quarterly Journal of the Geological Society* 69, no. March (1913): 117-51.

Deleuze, Gilles, and Félix Guattari. "1440: The Smooth and the Striated." In *A Thousand Plateaus: Capitalism and Schizophrenia*, 474-500. London: Athlone, 1988.

———. *A Thousand Plateaus: Capitalism and Schizophrenia*. London: Athlone, 1988.

Derrida, Jacques. *Writing and Difference*. Translated by Alan Bass. London: Routledge, 2001.

DeSilvey, Caitlin, and Tim Edensor. "Reckoning with Ruins." *Progress in Human Geography* (November 27, 2012 2012).

Dictionary, Macquarie. ""Resemblance"." Macmillan, https://www.macquariedictionary.com.au/features/word/

search/?word=resemblance&search_word_type=Dictionary.

Dictionary, Merriam-Webster. ""Resemblance"." Merriam-Webster, http://www.merriam-webster.com/dictionary/resemblance.

Dictionary, Oxford English. ""Resemblance"." Oxford University Press, http://www.oed.com/view/Entry/163464?rskey=S6pOIM&result=1.

Dillon, Sarah. *The Palimpsest: Literature, Criticism, Theory*. London: Continuum, 2007.

———. "Reinscribing De Quincey's Palimpsest: The Significance of the Palimpsest in Contemporary Literary and Cultural Studies." *Textual Practice* 19, no. 3 (2005/01/01 2005): 243-63.

Dixon, Susan M. "The Sources and Fortunes of Piranesi's Archaeological Illustrations." In *Tracing Architecture : The Aesthetics of Antiquarianism*, edited by Dana Arnold and Stephen Bending. Oxford: Blackwell, 2003.

Dorst, Kees, and Judith Dijkhuis. "Comparing Paradigms for Describing Design Activity." *Design Studies* 16, no. 2 (4// 1995): 261-74.

Drewett, Peter. *Field Archaeology: An Introduction*. London: UCL Press, 1999.

Eisenman, Peter. "Visions Unfolding: Architecture in the Age of Electronic Media." In *The Digital Turn in Architecture 1992-2012*, edited by Mario Carpo, 16-22. Chichester: Wiley, 2012 [1992].

Enger, Eldon D., Frederick C. Ross, and David B. Bailey. *Concepts in Biology.* 13th ed. New York: McGraw-Hill Higher Education, 2009.

The Church Commissioners of the Church of England. "Confirmation of a Supplementary Scheme Dealing with the Church of Saint

Swithun." Westminster, London: The Church of England, 1958.

Evans, Robin. *The Projective Cast: Architecture and Its Three Geometries*. Cambridge, Mass.: MIT Press, 1995.

Fabyan, Robert. *[the Chronicles of Fabyan.] Begin. [Fol. A 1, Preceded by Ten Leaves Containing the Heraldic Frontispiece and the Table,] Prima Pars Cronecarum. For That in the Accomptynge of the Yeres of the Worlde, Etc. End. Thus Endeth the Newe Cronycles of Englande and of Fraunce, Etc. B.L.* [London]: R. Pynson, 1516.

Fodor, Jerry A., and Massimo Piattelli-Palmarini. *What Darwin Got Wrong*. London: Profile, 2010.

Forsythe, William. "Choreographic Objects." Chap. 7 In *William Forsythe and the Practice of Choreography: It Starts from Any Point*, edited by Steven Spier, 90-92. Abingdon: Routledge, 2011.

Frascari, Marco. "Models and Drawings: The Invisible Nature of Architecture." In *2nd Annual AHRA International Conference: Models & Drawings: The Invisible Nature of Architecture*. University of Nottingham, UK, 2005.

———. ""Semiotica Ab Edendo," Taste in Architecture." *Journal of Architectural Education* (1984-) 40, no. 1 (1986): 2-7.

Frascari, Marco, and William Braham. "On the Mantic Paradigm in Architecture: The Projective Evocation of Future Edifices." *Proceedings of the Association of Collegiate Schools of Architecture Annual Meeting* (1994): 261-67.

Fraser, Antonia. *A History of Toys*. London: Spring Books, 1972.

Freud, Sigmund. "The 'Uncanny' (1919)." In *Art and Literature : Jensen's*

Gradiva, Leonardo Da Vinci and Other Works, edited by Albert Dickson, 335-76. Harmondsworth: Penguin, 1985.

Frodeman, Robert. *The Oxford Handbook of Interdisciplinarity*. Oxford: Oxford University Press, 2010.

Geertz, Clifford. *Local Knowledge : Further Essays in Interpretive Anthropology*. London: Fontana, 1993, 1983.

Gell, Alfred. *Art and Agency: An Anthropological Theory*. Oxford: Clarendon, 1998.

Gentner, Dedre. "Structure-Mapping: A Theoretical Framework for Analogy." *Cognitive Science* 7, no. 2 (1983): 155-70.

Gero, Joan M. "Honoring Ambiguity/Problematizing Certitude." *Journal of Archaeological Method and Theory* 14, no. 3 (2007): 311-27.

Giddens, Anthony. *The Constitution of Society: Outline of the Theory of Structuration*. Cambridge: Polity, 1984.

Glanville, Ranulph. "Researching Design and Designing Research." *Design Issues* 15, no. 2 (1999): 80-91.

Glapthorne, Henry. "Wit in a Constable [1639]." In *The Plays and Poems of Henry Glapthorne, Now First Collected with Illustrative Notes and a Memoir of the Author* [by R. H. Shepherd]. L.P, edited by Richard Herne Shepherd: 2 vol. J. Pearson: London, 1874.

Glendinning, Miles. *Modern Architect: The Life and Times of Robert Matthew*. London: RIBA Pub., 2008.

Goodwin, Charles. "Professional Vision." *American Anthropologist* 96, no. 3 (1994): 606-33.

Gosden, Chris. *Anthropology and Archaeology: A Changing Relationship*. London: Routledge, 1999.

Graves, Robert. *The Greek Myths* Volume 2. [S.l.]: Penguin Books, 1955.

Greene, Kevin. *Archaeology: An Introduction*, Fourth Edition. 4th ed. ed. London: Routledge, 2002.

Greene, Kevin, and Tom Moore. *Archaeology: An Introduction*, Fifth Edition. 5th ed. London: Routledge, 2010.

Grimm, Jacob, and Wilhelm Grimm. *Deutsches WöRterbuch*. Leipzig,: S. Hirzel, 1854.

Grosz, Elizabeth. *Architecture from the Outside : Essays on Virtual and Real Space*. Cambridge, Mass. ; [Great Britain]: MIT Press, 2001.

Guattari, Felix. "Transversality." Translated by Rosemary Sheed. In *Molecular Revolution: Psychiatry and Politics*, edited by Felix Guattari, 11-23. Harmondsworth: Penguin, 1984.

Gurevich, Aron. "The French Historical Revolution: The Annales School." In *Interpreting Archaeology : Finding Meaning in the Past*, edited by Ian Hodder, vii, 275p. London: Routledge, 1995.

GVA, and Purcell Miller Tritton LLP. "London Stone Relocation: PPS5 Statement." London, 2011.

Halliwell-Phillipps, James Orchard. *A Treatyse of a Galaunt; with the Maryage of the Fayre Pusell, the Bosse of Byllyngesgate Unto London Stone*. [in Verse.] from the Unique Edition Printed by Wynkyn De Worde. Edited by J. O. H. London, 1860 [1522].

Hambly, Maya. *Drawing Instruments 1580-1980*. London: Sotheby's

Publications, 1988.

Haughton, William. *English-Men for My Money; or, a Pleasant Comedy, Called a Woman Will Have Her Will.* [by W. H.]. 1616.

Hawthorne, Nathaniel. *The English Notebooks, Based Upon the Original Manuscripts in the Pierpont Morgan Library*. New York: Modern Language Association of America, 1941.

Heddon, Deirdre, Carl Lavery, and Phil Smith. *Walking, Writing and Performance: Autobiographical Texts*. Bristol: Intellect Books, 2009.

Heritage., English. "Heritage Listing: London Stone." English Heritage, http://list.english-heritage.org.uk/resultsingle.aspx?uid=1286846.

Hesiod. *Hesiod, the Homeric Hymns and Homerica*. [S.l.]: Heinemann, 1914.

Hesse, Mary Brenda. *Models and Analogies in Science*. pp. 150. Sheed & Ward: London & New York, 1963.

———. "Models Versus Paradigms in the Natural Sciences." In *The Use of Models in the Social Sciences*, edited by Lyndhurst Collins, 1-15. London: Tavistock Publications, 1976.

———. "On Defining Analogy." *Proceedings of the Aristotelian Society* 60 (1959): 79-100.

Hill, Jonathan. *The Illegal Architect*. London: Black Dog, 1998.

———. "Institutions of Architecture." *Offramp: detours and dialogues* 7, no. 1 (2000): 73-81.

"The History of Birkbeck." Birkbeck, University of London, http://www.

bbk.ac.uk/about-us/history.

Hodder, Ian. "Field Team." http://www.catalhoyuk.com/team/.

———, ed. *Symbolic and Structural Archaeology*. Cambridge: Cambridge University Press, 2006.

———. *Towards Reflexive Method in Archaeology: The Example at Çatalhöyük*. Cambridge: McDonald Institute for Archaeological Research, 2000.

Homer, E. V. Rieu, D. C. H. Rieu, and P. V. Jones. *The Iliad* [in Translated from the Ancient Greek.]. [Rev. ed.] / revised and updated by Peter Jones with D.C.H. Rieu / edited with an introduction and notes by Peter Jones. ed. London: Penguin, 2003.

Hope-Taylor, Brian. "Archaeological Draughtsmanship: Principles and Practice. Part Ii: Ends and Means." *Antiquity* 40, no. 158 (1966): 107-13.

Ingold, Tim. *Making: Anthropology, Archaeology, Art and Architecture*. 2013.

———, ed. *Redrawing Anthropology: Materials, Movements, Lines*. Farnham: Ashgate, 2011.

Ancient Monuments and Archaeological Areas Act 1979.

Planning (Listed Buildings and Conservation Areas) Act 1990.

Irving, Washington. *The Sketch Book of Geoffrey Crayon, Gent.* Second Edition. London: John Murray, 1820.

James, Simon. "Drawing Inferences: Visual Reconstructions in Theory and Practice." In *The Cultural Life of Images : Visual Representation in Archaeology*, edited by Brian Molyneaux. London ; New York: Routledge, 1997.

James, William. *Pragmatism. The Works of William James*. Cambridge, Mass.: Harvard University Press, 1975 [1907].

Jentsch, Ernst. "On the Psychology of the Uncanny (1906) 1." *Angelaki* 2, no. 1 (1997/01/01 1997): 7-16.

John, David Gethin. *Images of Goethe through Schiller's Egmont* [in Includes German text of Egmont.]. Montreal ; London: McGill-Queen's University Press, 1998.

Jones, John Chris. *Design Methods*. 2nd ed.: Van Nost. Reinhold, 1992.

Jones, Michael Christopher Emlyn, C.T. Allmand, John Benet, G. L. Harriss, and M. A. Harriss. *The Camden Miscellany*. Vol. 24. London: Offices of the Royal Historical Society, 1972.

Klein, J.T. "A Conceptual Vocabulary of Interdisciplinary Science." In *Practising Interdisciplinarity*, edited by Peter Ed Weingart and Nico Ed Stehr: University of Toronto Press, 2000.

Knight, Mark. "Must Farm: Must Read." Cambridge: Cambridge Archaeological Unit, 2012.

Kobayashi, Masaomi. "The Pursuit of Interdisciplinarities: A Critique of Cultural Studies." In *University of the Ryukyus Repository*, 167-75: University of the Ryukyus, 2006.

Koldewey, Robert. Das Wieder Erstehende Babylon. Die Bisherigen Ergebnisse Der Deutschen Ausgrabungen ... Mit 255 Abbildungen Und Planen, Davon 7 in *Farbigem Lichtdruck*. pp. vii. 328. 1913., 1913.

Kristeva, Julia. "Institutional Interdisciplinarity in Theory and in Practice: An Interview." In *De-, Dis-, Ex-. Vol.2, Anxiety of Interdisciplinarity*, edited by Alex Coles and Alexia Defert, pp.2-22. London: BACKless Books in association with Black Dog Publishing, 1998.

Lacan, Jacques. *Anxiety: The Seminar of Jacques Lacan*, Book X. Cambridge: Polity Press, 2014.

Lambert, B. *The History and Survey of London and Its Environs : From the Earliest Period to the Present Time*. [S.l.]: T. Hughes, 1806.

Latour, Bruno. *Pandora's Hope : Essays on the Reality of Science Studies*. Cambridge, Mass. ; London: Harvard University Press, 1999.

———. "A Well-Articulated Primatology: Reflexions of a Fellow Traveller." Chap. 17 In *Primate Encounters: Models of Science, Gender, and Society*, edited by Shirley Strum and Linda Marie Fedigan, 358-81. Chicago ; London: University of Chicago Press, 2000.

Lawson, Bryan. *How Designers Think: The Design Process Demystified*. 4th ed. Amsterdam; London: Architectural Press [Elsevier], 2006.

Lemke, Matt. "Give Me Whs or Give Me Death!". *Assemblage*, no. 2 (2nd May 1997).

Lévi-Strauss, Claude. *The Elementary Structures of Kinship*. Translated by James Harle Bell and John Richard von Sturmer. London: Eyre & Spottiswoode, 1969 [1949].

Lofting, Hugh. *The Story of Doctor Dolittle, Being the History of His Peculiar Life at Home and Astonishing Adventures in Foreign Parts*. New York,: Frederick A. Stokes Company, 1920.

———. *The Voyages of Doctor Dolittle*. New York,: Fredk. A. Stokes co.,

1922.

Love, Serena. "Architecture as Material Culture: Building Form and Materiality in the Pre-Pottery Neolithic of Anatolia and Levant." *Journal of Anthropological Archaeology* 32 (2013): 746-58.

Lovejoy, Arthur O. *The Great Chain of Being: A Study of the History of an Idea*. Somerset, N.J.: Transaction, 2009.

Lucas, Gavin. "Fast Ruins. Nature and Modernity in Iceland." In *Ruin Memories*, 2011.

Macdonald, Sharon. *A Companion to Museum Studies*. Chicester: Wiley-Blackwell, 2011.

Mahoney, Edward P. "Lovejoy and the Hierarchy of Being." *Journal of the History of Ideas* 48, no. 2 (1987): 211-30.

Maitland, Frederic William. *The Collected Papers of Frederic William Maitland*. edited by H. A. L. Fisher Cambridge: University Press, 1911.

The Worshipful Company of Spectacle Makers. "Minute of 1671 Records." The Worshipful Company of Spectacle Makers, http://www.spectaclemakers.com/contact/index.htm.

Marsden, Peter. "The Excavation of a Roman Palace Site in London, 1961-1972." *Transactions of the London and Middlesex Archaeological Society* 26 (1975): 1-102.

McFadyen, Lesley. "Practice Drawing Writing Object." In *Redrawing Anthropology : Materials, Movements, Lines*, edited by Tim Ingold. Farnham: Ashgate, 2011.

McNabb, John. "The Lying Stones of Sussex: An Investigation into the Role of the Flint Tools in the Development of the Piltdown Forgery."

Archaeological Journal 163 (2006): 1-41.

Meece, Stephanie. "A Bird's Eye View - of a Leopard's Spots. The Çatalhöyük 'Map' and the Development of Cartographic Representation in Prehistory.". *Anatolian Studies* 56 (2006): 1-16.

Merrion, Mor [Richard Williams Morgan]. "Stonehenge." *Notes and Queries* 3rd Series Vol.1 (1862).

Moloney, N., and Michael J. Shott, eds. *Lithic Analysis at the Millennium*. London: Institute of Archaeology, University College London, 2003.

Moore, Henrietta. "The Problems of Origins: Poststructuralism and Beyond." In *Interpreting Archaeology : Finding Meaning in the Past*, edited by Ian Hodder, M. Shanks, Alexandra Alexandri, Victor Buchli, John Carman, Jonathan Last and Gavin Lucas, 51-53. London: Routledge, 1995.

Moshenska, Gabriel. "Institute of Archaeology Celebrates." *British Archaeology*, no. 124 (May/June 2012).

Nichols, Deborah L., Rosemary A. Joyce, and Susan D. Gillespie. "Is Archaeology Anthropology?". In *Archaeology Is Anthropology*, edited by Susan D. Gillespie and Deborah L. Nichols: American Anthropological Association, 2003.

O'Connor, Blaze. "Dust and Debitage: An Archaeology of Francis Bacon's Studio." In *Archaeologies of Art: Papers from the Sixth World Archaeological Congress*, 2-9. University College Dublin: UCD Scholarcast, 2008.

Parker Pearson, M., and C. Richards. "Ordering the World: Perceptions of Architecture, Space and Time." In *Architecture and Order :*

Approaches to Social Space, edited by Michael Parker Pearson and Colin Richards. London: Routledge, 1994.

Pearson, Mike, and Michael Shanks. *Theatre/Archaeology*. London: Routledge, 2001.

Peirce, Charles S. *Pragmatism and Pragmaticism*. Bristol: Thoemmes, 1998.

Peirce, Charles S., and Carolyn Eisele. *The New Elements of Mathematics*. The Hague: Mouton [etc], 1976.

Pennant, Thomas. *Some Account of London*. [Another edition.] Third edition. ed.: London, 1793.

Pérez-Gómez, Alberto, and Louise Pelletier. *Architectural Representation and the Perspective Hinge*. Cambridge, Mass.; London: MIT Press, 2000 [1997].

Perry, Sara. "Crafting Knowledge with (Digital) Visual Media in Archaeology." In *Material Evidence: Learning from Archaeological Practice*, edited by Robert Chapman and Alison Wylie, 189-210. Abingdon and New York: Routledge, 2015.

Phillips, Philip. "American Archaeology and General Anthropological Theory." *Southwestern Journal of Anthropology* 11, no. 3 (1955): 246-50.

Picon, Antoine. *French Architects and Engineers in the Age of Enlightenment*. Cambridge: Cambridge University Press, 1992.

Pistis, Marco. "From Caveat Emptor to Caveat Venditor - a Brief History of English Sale of Goods Law." *Mondaq*, http://bit.ly/1LgfJUz.

Pred, Allan. "The Choreography of Existence: Comments on Hägerstrand's Time-Geography and Its Usefulness." *Economic*

Geography 53, no. 2 (1977): 207-21.

Presner, Todd Samuel. ""What a Synoptic and Artificial View Reveals": Extreme History and the Modernism of W. G. Sebald's Realism." *Criticism* 46, no. 3 (2004): 341-60.

Price, John Edward. A *Description of the Roman Tessellated Pavement Found in Bucklersbury : With Observations on Analogous Discoveries.* Westminster: Nichols and Sons, 1870.

Ranke, Leopold von. *Geschichten Der Romanischen Und Germanischen Völker Von 1494 Bis 1514* [in German]. Leipzig: Duncker & Humblot, 1885 [1824].

Rendell, Jane. "Cut on the Bias: Relating Art and Architecture through Interdisciplinarity and Transdisciplinarity." In *Art Et Architecture*, edited by Marie Ange Brayer. Orléans: Editions HYX, 2013.

———. "From Architectural History to Spatial Writing." In *Rethinking Architectural Historiography*, edited by Dana Arnold, Elvan Altan Ergut and Belgin Turan Özkaya, xx, 251 p. London: Routledge, 2006.

———. "Walking Backwards through Brassai." http://www.janerendell.co.uk/walks/walking-backwards-through-brassai.

———. "Walking to Wapping/ Walking through Angels." http://www.janerendell.co.uk/walks/walking-backwards-through-brassai.

Renfrew, Colin. "The Great Tradition Versus the Great Divide: Archaeology as Anthropology?". *American Journal of Archaeology* 84, no. 3 (1980): 287-98.

Richardson, Lorna. "Prescot Street: What Tools Do Archaeologists Use?" L-P Archaeology.

Robbins, Edward. *Why Architects Draw*. Cambridge, Mass.; London: MIT Press, 1994.

Robinson, Fitzroy. 25th March 1960.

Rowland, Ingrid D. "Raphael, Angelo Colocci, and the Genesis of the Architectural Orders." *The Art Bulletin* 76, no. 1 (1994): 81-104.

Rudofsky, Bernard. *Architecture without Architects: A Short Introduction to Non-Pedigree Architecture*. Albuquerque: University of New Mexico Press, 1964.

Rykwert, Joseph. *The Necessity of Artifice : Ideas in Architecture*. London: Academy Editions, 1982.

Saint, Andrew. *Architect and Engineer: A Study in Sibling Rivalry*. New Haven, Conn. ; London: Yale University Press, 2008.

Schaik, Leon van, ed. *Ruins of the Future: Site Works from Ruins of the Future Competition, Adelaide Festival*. Melbourne: RMIT, 2000.

Schnapp, Alain. *The Discovery of the Past: The Origins of Archaeology*. London: British Museum Press, 1996.

Schön, Donald A. *The Reflective Practitioner: How Professionals Think in Action.* New York : Basic Books, 1983.

Sennett, Richard. *The Craftsman*. London: Allen Lane, 2008.

Shakespeare, William. *The First Part of the Contention: The First Quarto, 1594*. edited by Frederick James Furnivall and Richard Grant White London: C. Praetorius, 1594.

———. *Mr William Shakespeares Comedies, Histories & Tragedies*. Published According to the True Originall Copies. London: 3 pt. Isaac

Iaggard and Ed. Blount, 1623 [reprinted 1807].

Shanks, M., and Ian Hodder. "Processual, Postprocessual and Interpretive Archaeologies." In *Interpreting Archaeology: Finding Meaning in the Past*, edited by Ian Hodder, M. Shanks, Alexandra Alexandri, Victor Buchli, John Carman, Jonathan Last and Gavin Lucas, 3-29. London: Routledge, 1995.

Shanks, Michael. "Anglo-American-Antiquarians." http://stanford.io/XVdr11.

———. "In Design There's Never a Clean Slate." In *Michael Shanks: all things archaeological*, edited by Michael Shanks. Stanford, 2014.

———. "Michael Shanks: Nine Archaeological Theses on Design." http://documents.stanford.edu/michaelshanks/260.

Shanks, Michael, and Randall H. McGuire. "The Craft of Archaeology." *American Antiquity* 61, no. 1 (1996): 75-88.

Shanks, Michael, and Christopher Tilley. *Re-Constructing Archaeology: Theory and Practice*. London: Routledge, 1992.

Shanks, Michael, and Christopher Witmore. "Memory Practices and the Archaeological Imagination in Risk Society: Design and Long Term Community." Stanford University.

Shelley [uncredited in this 1st Edition], Mary Wollstonecraft. *Frankenstein: Or the Modern Prometheus*. 3 vols London: Lackington, Hughes, Harding, Mavor, & Jones, 1818.

Simon, Herbert A. *The Sciences of the Artificial*. 3rd ed. Cambridge, Mass.: MIT Press, 1996.

Smith, Albert C. *Architectural Model as Machine: A New View of Models from Antiquity to the Present Day*. Oxford: Architectural, 2004.

Smith, Laurajane. *Uses of Heritage*. London; New York: Routledge, 2006.

Smith, Phil. "Walking-Based Arts: A Resource for the Guided Tour?". *Scandinavian Journal of Hospitality and Tourism* 13, no. 2 (2013/06/01 2013): 103-14.

Smithson, Robert. "A Tour of the Monuments of Passaic, New Jersey." In *Robert Smithson: Writings of Robert Smithson*, edited by Jack D. Flam. Berkeley, Calif. ; London: University of California Press, 1996 [1967].

Sorrell, Alan. *Roman London*. London: B.T. Batsford, 1969.

Stafford, Barbara Maria. *Artful Science: Enlightenment, Entertainment and the Eclipse of Visual Education*. Cambridge, Mass. ; London: MIT Press, 1994.

———. "Barbara Maria Stafford: Bio." Barbara Maria Stafford, http://barbaramariastafford.com/curriculum-vitae-bio.html.

———. *Body Criticism: Imaging the Unseen in Enlightenment Art and Medicine*. Cambridge, Mass. ; London: MIT, 1991.

———. *Good Looking: Essays on the Virtue of Images*. Cambridge, Mass. ; London: MIT Press, 1996.

———. "Paying Attention: The Fine Art and Neuroscience of Visual Awareness." *The Comparison Project,* Drake University, https://comparisonproject.wordpress.drake.edu.

———. *Visual Analogy: Consciousness as the Art of Connecting*.

Cambridge, Mass. ; London: MIT Press, 1999.

Stafford, Barbara Maria, and Frances Terpak. *Devices of Wonder: From the World in a Box to Images on a Screen*. Los Angeles, Calif. ; [Great Britain]: Getty Research Institute, 2001.

Stanley-Price, Nicholas. "The Reconstruction of Ruins: Principles and Practice." In *Archaeological Sites : Conservation and Management*, edited by Sharon Sullivan and Richard Mackay, 514-27. Los Angeles: Getty Conservation Institute, 2012.

Stow, John, and John Strype. *A Survey of the Cities of London and Westminster : Containing the Original, Antiquity, Increase, Modern Estate and Government of Those Cities*. London ; 1720., 1720.

Stow, John, and William John Thoms. A Survey of London. *A survey of London*, written in the year 1598. A new edition, edited by William J. Thoms. ed.: London, 1842 [1598].

Street, C. E. Earthstars: *The Visionary Landscape*. London: Hermitage, 2000.

Stukeley, William. "Commonplace Book." edited by Wiltshire Heritage Museum Wiltshire Archaeological and Natural History Society Library, Devizes, 1717-.

Thomas, Julian. "On the Ocularcentrism of Archaeology." In *Archaeology and the Politics of Vision in a Post-Modern Context*, edited by Julian Thomas and Vitor Oliveira Jorge. Newcastle upon Tyne: Cambridge Scholars Publishing, 2008.

Tufte, Edward R. *The Visual Display of Quantitative Information*. Cheshire, Conn.: Graphics Press, 1983.

Tyers, P. A. "Potsherd:Atlas of Roman Pottery." http://potsherd.net/atlas/topics/tools.

Vansina, Jan. "Historians, Are Archeologists Your Siblings?". *History in Africa* 22 (1995): 369-408.

Vesely, Dalibor. "Architecture and the Conflict of Representation." *AA Files* 8 (1985): 21-38.

Weiner, J. S. *The Piltdown Forgery*. 50th anniversary ed. Oxford: Oxford University Press, 2003.

Williams Morgan, Richard [RWM]. "London Stone, Cannon Street." *Notes and Queries* 2nd Series Vol.5 (1858).

Williams, Raymond. *Marxism and Literature*. Oxford: Oxford University Press, 1977.

Wittgenstein, Ludwig. *Philosophical Investigations* [in Parallel German and English text with Latin passages.]. 2nd ed.. Oxford : Blackwell, 1958 (1997 [printing]), 1958.

Wright, David. "Church of St. Swithin's London Stone." Geograph, http://www.geograph.org.uk/photo/1031034.

Yablon, Nick. *Untimely Ruins: An Archaeology of American Urban Modernity, 1819-1919*. Chicago: University of Chicago Press, 2009.

Yeomans, John. "What's Happening with London Stone?" *Londonist* [online], 2012.

Zambelli, Alessandro. "Occlusions of the Operational Sequence: A Coincidental Conversation between Robert Matthew and André Leroi-Gourhan in 6 Diagrams." *Architectural Theory Review* 21, no. 2 (2017): 149-71.

———. "Occlusions of the Operational Sequence: A Coincidental Conversation between Robert Matthew and André Leroi-Gourhan in Six Diagrams." In *Architecture and Anthropology*, edited by Adam Jasper. London: Routledge, 2018.

———. "The Undisciplined Drawing." *Buildings* 3, no. 2 (2013): 357-79.

———. "Villa Madama and the Scandalous Practice of Raffaello Sanzio." In *'Looking Before and After': Cultural Exchange and the Inheritance of Ideas c.1200-c.1700*. Christ Church College, University of Oxford, 2009.

Notes

1 The real name of John (Jack) Cade is unclear. During the rebellion he claimed to be called John Mortimer and there is speculation that he did this to suggest a kinship with Richard Mortimer, Duke of York which he did not have. It is also possible that this was his real name. There are contemporaneous and near-contemporaneous accounts of Cade's rebellion of 1450 and the events at London Stone on 3rd July of that year. The 1594 First Quarto edition of Shakespeare's play recounts that London Stone was struck by Cade with his sword and this accords with those eye-witness accounts. The more commonly used 1623 First Folio version has him strike the Stone with his staff. See: John Clark, "Jack Cade at London Stone," *Transactions of the London and Middlesex Archaeological Society* 58(2007): 181.; William Shakespeare, *The First Part of the Contention: The First Quarto, 1594*, ed. Frederick James Furnivall and Richard Grant White (London: C. Praetorius, 1594).; and *Mr William Shakespeares Comedies, Histories & Tragedies. Published According to the True Originall Copies* (London: 3 pt. Isaac Iaggard and Ed. Blount, 1623 [reprinted 1807]).

2 Anon., "The Cannon Street Stall-Keeper," *The Daily Graphic*, 24 April 1901.

3 Clark, "Jack Cade at London Stone."

4 Edward Hallett Carr, *What Is History?: The George Macaulay Trevelyan Lectures Delivered in the University of Cambridge January-March 1961* (Harmondsworth: Penguin, 1987), 11.

5 Jan Vansina, "Historians, Are Archeologists Your Siblings?," *History in Africa* 22(1995): 370.

6 Barbara Maria Stafford, *Visual Analogy: Consciousness as the Art of Connecting* (Cambridge, Mass. ; London: MIT Press, 1999), 8. Stafford perhaps misquoting James F. Anderson's English translation of Paul Grenet's French translation of Plato.

7 Tim Ingold, *Making: Anthropology, Archaeology, Art and Architecture* (2013), 10.

8 Aron Gurevich, "The French Historical Revolution: The Annales School," in *Interpreting Archaeology : Finding Meaning in the Past*, ed. Ian Hodder (London: Routledge, 1995), 159.

9 Leopold von Ranke, *Geschichten Der Romanischen Und Germanischen Völker Von 1494 Bis 1514* (Leipzig: Duncker & Humblot, 1885 [1824]).

10 Todd Samuel Presner, ""What a Synoptic and Artificial View Reveals": Extreme History and the Modernism of W. G. Sebald's Realism," *Criticism* 46, no. 3 (2004): 343.

11 Walter Benjamin, *The Arcades Project*, trans. Howard Eiland and Kevin McLaughlin (Cambridge, Mass. ; London: Belknap Press, 1999), 463.

12 Carr, *What Is History?: The George Macaulay Trevelyan Lectures Delivered in the University of Cambridge January-March 1961*, 23.

13 Ian Hodder, ed. *Symbolic and Structural Archaeology* (Cambridge: Cambridge University Press, 2006). and: M. Shanks and Ian Hodder, "Processual, Postprocessual and Interpretive Archaeologies," in *Interpreting Archaeology: Finding Meaning in the Past*, ed. Ian Hodder, et al. (London: Routledge, 1995).

14 Ian Hodder, *Towards Reflexive Method in Archaeology: The Example at Çatalhöyük* (Cambridge: McDonald Institute for Archaeological Research, 2000).

15 "Cotúa Island-Orinoco Reflexive Archaeology Project," UCL Institute of Archaeology, http://www.ucl.ac.uk/archaeology/research/directory/orinoco-reflexive-oliver.

16 Bernard Rudofsky, *Architecture without Architects: A Short Introduction to Non-Pedigree Architecture* (Albuquerque: University of New Mexico Press, 1964).

17 Bruno Latour, "A Well-Articulated Primatology: Reflexions of a Fellow Traveller," in *Primate Encounters: Models of Science, Gender, and Society*, ed. Shirley Strum and Linda Marie Fedigan (Chicago ; London: University of Chicago Press, 2000), 15.

18 For example: Michael Shanks and Christopher Tilley, *Re-Constructing Archaeology: Theory and Practice* (London: Routledge, 1992). and; Michael Shanks and Christopher Witmore, "Memory Practices and the Archaeological Imagination in *Risk Society: Design and Long Term Community*," Stanford University.

19 Nicholas Stanley-Price, "The Reconstruction of Ruins: Principles and Practice," in *Archaeological Sites : Conservation and Management*, ed. Sharon Sullivan and Richard Mackay (Los Angeles: Getty Conservation Institute, 2012), 522.

20 Joan M. Gero, "Honoring Ambiguity/Problematizing Certitude," *Journal of Archaeological Method and Theory* 14, no. 3 (2007): 311.

21 Kevin Greene and Tom Moore, *Archaeology: An Introduction*, Fifth Edition, 5th ed. (London: Routledge, 2010), 135.

22 Throughout this book the term interdisciplinary is used to

define general aspects of practice between disciplines except where the transgressive movement between disciplines is being emphasised. In these cases, the term transdisciplinary is preferred.

23 Claude Lévi-Strauss, *The Elementary Structures of Kinship*, trans. James Harle Bell and John Richard von Sturmer (London: Eyre & Spottiswoode, 1969 [1949]).

24 Robert Smithson, "A Tour of the Monuments of Passaic, New Jersey," in *Robert Smithson: Writings of Robert Smithson*, ed. Jack D. Flam (Berkeley, Calif. ; London: University of California Press, 1996 [1967]), 54.

25 See for example: Leon van Schaik, ed. *Ruins of the Future: Site Works from Ruins of the Future Competition, Adelaide Festival* (Melbourne: RMIT, 2000).; Nick Yablon, *Untimely Ruins: An Archaeology of American Urban Modernity*, 1819-1919 (Chicago: University of Chicago Press, 2009).; Caitlin DeSilvey and Tim Edensor, "Reckoning with Ruins," *Progress in Human Geography* (2012). and; Gavin Lucas to Ruin Memories, 20.3.13, 2011, http://ruinmemories.org/modern-ruins-of-iceland/fast-ruins-nature-and-modernity-in-iceland/.

26 The first version was linear – the circularity and omni-directional arrows are later addition.

27 Smithson, "A Tour of the Monuments of Passaic, New Jersey," 56.

28 Julia Kristeva, "Institutional Interdisciplinarity in Theory and in Practice: An Interview," in *De-, Dis-, Ex-. Vol.2, Anxiety of Interdisciplinarity*, ed. Alex Coles and Alexia Defert (London: BACKless Books in association with Black Dog Publishing, 1998), 5.

29 The diagram shows nine site of encounter, 1-7 are with archaeology, A and B with anthropology and art practice respectively.

30 *Certificate in Archaeology of the Palaeolithic and Mesolithic Periods*, Birkbeck, University of London, Faculty of Continuing Education, 2003-2004 taught by Dr. Norah Moloney.

31 Gabriel Moshenska, "Institute of Archaeology Celebrates," *British Archaeology*, no. 124 (2012).

32 "The History of Birkbeck," Birkbeck, University of London, http://www.bbk.ac.uk/about-us/history.

33 See for example; N. Moloney and Michael J. Shott, eds., *Lithic Analysis at the Millennium* (London: Institute of Archaeology, University College London, 2003).

34 Ernst Jentsch, "On the Psychology of the Uncanny (1906) 1," *Angelaki* 2, no. 1 (1997).

35 Sigmund Freud, "The 'Uncanny' (1919)," in *Art and Literature : Jensen's Gradiva, Leonardo Da Vinci and Other Works*, ed. Albert Dickson (Harmondsworth: Penguin, 1985).

36 Ibid., 345.

37 Ibid. Freud quotes Schelling from Daniel Sanders's *Wörterbuch der Deutschen Sprache*.

38 Ibid.

39 Ibid., 371.

40 Brian Hope-Taylor, "Archaeological Draughtsmanship: Principles and Practice. Part Ii: Ends and Means," *Antiquity* 40, no. 158 (1966): 110-12.

41 Jane Rendell, "Cut on the Bias: Relating Art and Architecture through Interdisciplinarity and Transdisciplinarity," in *Art Et Architecture*, ed. Marie Ange Brayer (Orléans: Editions HYX, 2013 [forthcoming]),

42 Alex Coles and Alexia Defert, De-, Dis-, Ex-. Vol.2, *Anxiety*

of Interdisciplinarity (London: BACKless Books in association with Black Dog Publishing, 1998), 162.

43 Donald T. Campbell, "Ethnocentrism of Disciplines and the Fish-Scale Model of Omniscience," in *Interdisciplinary Relationships in the Social Sciences*, ed. Muzafer Sherif and Carolyn W. Sherif (Somerset, N.J.: AldineTransaction ; London : Eurospan [distributor], 2009), 6.

A thorough and more contemporary account of interdisciplinarity in and amongst science disciplines can be found in; Andrew Barry and Georgina Born, "Interdisciplinarity: Reconfigurations of the Social and Natural Sciences," in *Interdisciplinarity: Reconfigurations of the Social and Natural Sciences*, ed. Andrew Barry and Georgina Born (London; New York, NY: Routledge, 2013).

44 Campbell, "Ethnocentrism of Disciplines and the Fish-Scale Model of Omniscience," 329.

45 A problem not entirely solved even today; the first chapter of *The Oxford Handbook of Interdisciplinarity. A Short History of Knowledge Formations*, deals almost exclusively with hard and social sciences. See; Robert Frodeman, *The Oxford Handbook of Interdisciplinarity* (Oxford: Oxford University Press, 2010).

46 Campbell, "Ethnocentrism of Disciplines and the Fish-Scale Model of Omniscience," 8.

47 Craig Bremner and Paul Rodgers, "Design without Discipline," *Design Issues* 29, no. 3 (2013).

48 John Chris Jones, *Design Methods*, 2nd ed. (Van Nost. Reinhold, 1992).

49 Nigel Cross, *Designerly Ways of Knowing* (London: Springer, 2006).

50 Michael M. Crow and William B. Dabars, *Designing the New American University* (Baltimore: Johns Hopkins University Press, 2015), 197.

51 J.T. Klein, "A Conceptual Vocabulary of Interdisciplinary Science," in *Practising Interdisciplinarity*, ed. Peter Ed Weingart and Nico Ed Stehr (University of Toronto Press, 2000).

52 Alex Coles and Defert, De-, Dis-, Ex-. Vol.2, *Anxiety of Interdisciplinarity*.

53 Claude Lévi-Strauss, *The Elementary Structures of Kinship*, trans. James Harle Bell and John Richard von Sturmer (London: Eyre & Spottiswoode, 1969 [1949]).

54 Elizabeth Grosz, *Architecture from the Outside : Essays on Virtual and Real Space* (Cambridge, Mass. ; [Great Britain]: MIT Press, 2001), xvi.

55 Bruno Latour, *Pandora's Hope : Essays on the Reality of Science Studies* (Cambridge, Mass. ; London: Harvard University Press, 1999), 309.

56 Grosz, *Architecture from the Outside : Essays on Virtual and Real Space*, xvi.

57 Julia Kristeva, "Institutional Interdisciplinarity in Theory and in Practice: An Interview," in *De-, Dis-, Ex-. Vol.2, Anxiety of Interdisciplinarity*, ed. Alex Coles and Alexia Defert (London: BACKless Books in association with Black Dog Publishing, 1998), 5.

58 Jane Rendell, "From Architectural History to Spatial Writing," in *Rethinking Architectural Historiography*, ed. Dana Arnold, Elvan Altan Ergut, and Belgin Turan Özkaya (London: Routledge, 2006), 135-37.

59 Rendell, "Cut on the Bias: Relating Art and Architecture

through Interdisciplinarity and Transdisciplinarity.", p. unknown..

60 Bremner and Rodgers, "Design without Discipline," 11.

61 Alex Coles and Alexia Defert, "Introduction," in *De-, Dis-, Ex-. Vol.2, Anxiety of Interdisciplinarity*, ed. Alex Coles and Alexia Defert (London: BACKless Books in association with Black Dog Publishing, 1998), i.

62 Klein, "A Conceptual Vocabulary of Interdisciplinary Science," 7.

63 Gilles Deleuze and Félix Guattari, *A Thousand Plateaus: Capitalism and Schizophrenia* (London: Athlone, 1988), 381.

64 Julia Kristeva, "Institutional Interdisciplinarity in Theory and in Practice: An Interview," 5.

65 Ibid., 6.

66 Felix Guattari, "Transversality," in *Molecular Revolution: Psychiatry and Politics*, ed. Felix Guattari (Harmondsworth: Penguin, 1984), 17.

67 Jane Rendell, "Cut on the Bias: Relating Art and Architecture through Interdisciplinarity and Transdisciplinarity," in *Art Et Architecture*, ed. Marie Ange Brayer (Orléans: Editions HYX, 2013)., p. unknown.

68 Sarah Dillon, "Reinscribing De Quincey's Palimpsest: The Significance of the Palimpsest in Contemporary Literary and Cultural Studies," *Textual Practice* 19, no. 3 (2005): 254.

69 Ibid.

70 *The Palimpsest: Literature, Criticism, Theory* (London: Continuum, 2007), 2.

71 Kristeva, "Institutional Interdisciplinarity in Theory and in Practice: An Interview," 5.

72 Ibid.

73 Masaomi Kobayashi, "The Pursuit of Interdisciplinarities: A Critique of Cultural Studies," in *University of the Ryukyus Repository* (University of the Ryukyus, 2006).

74 Alessandro Zambelli *International Journal of the Arts in Society*, Volume 5, Issue 6, pp.163-174

75 Mark Cousins, "Building an Architect," in *Occupying Architecture: Between the Architect and the User*, ed. Jonathan Hill (London: Routledge, 1998).

76 Alex Coles and Defert, "Introduction," iii.

77 Barbara Maria Stafford, *Visual Analogy: Consciousness as the Art of Connecting* (Cambridge, Mass. ; London: MIT Press, 1999), 82.

78 Michael Shanks and Christopher Tilley, *Re-Constructing Archaeology: Theory and Practice* (London: Routledge, 1992), xvii-xviii.

79 Ibid., 16.

80 accessed 26.04.10.

81 Shanks and Tilley, *Re-Constructing Archaeology: Theory and Practice*, 24.

82 Michael Shanks and Randall H. McGuire, "The Craft of Archaeology," *American Antiquity* 61, no. 1 (1996): 76.

83 Henrietta Moore, "The Problems of Origins: Poststructuralism and Beyond," in *Interpreting Archaeology : Finding Meaning in the Past*, ed. Ian Hodder, et al. (London: Routledge, 1995), 51.

84 Michael Shanks, "Anglo-American-Antiquarians," http://stanford.io/XVdr11. accessed 09.06.12.

85 Mike Pearson and Michael Shanks, *Theatre/Archaeology*

(London: Routledge, 2001), 3.

86 Richard Sennett, *The Craftsman* (London: Allen Lane, 2008), 8.

87 Ibid., 10.

88 Ibid., 9.

89 See for example; Sara Perry, "Crafting Knowledge with (Digital) Visual Media in Archaeology," in *Material Evidence: Learning from Archaeological Practice*, ed. Robert Chapman and Alison Wylie (Abingdon and New York: Routledge, 2015).

90 http://documents.stanford.edu/michaelshanks/Home, accessed 03.01.11.

91 Sennett, *The Craftsman,* 287.

92 Jonathan Bean and Daniela Rosner, "Old Hat: Craft Versus Design?," *ACM Interactions* January-February(2012): 86.

93 Ibid.

94 Shanks and McGuire, "The Craft of Archaeology," 77-78.

95 Michael Shanks and Tilley, *Re-Constructing Archaeology: Theory and Practice*, 243.

96 Jane Anderson, *Basics Architecture 03: Architectural Design* (Lausanne ; Worthing: AVA Academia, 2011), 36.

97 Post-processualism: "based on the notions that culture must be understood as sets of symbols that evoke meanings, and that these meanings vary depending on the particular contexts of use and the specific histories of both artifacts and the people who use them" Paul G. Bahn, *The Penguin Archaeology Guide*, Rev., expanded and updated ed. (London: Penguin, 2001), 365.

98 Bryan Lawson, *How Designers Think: The Design Process Demystified*, 4th ed. (Amsterdam; London: Architectural Press

[Elsevier], 2006), 4.

99 Donald A. Schön, *The Reflective Practitioner: How Professionals Think in Action* (New York : Basic Books, 1983), 76.

100 Herbert A. Simon, *The Sciences of the Artificial*, 3rd ed. (Cambridge, Mass.: MIT Press, 1996); Christopher Alexander, *Notes on the Synthesis of Form* (Cambridge, Mass.: Harvard University Press, 1964).

101 Ranulph Glanville, "Researching Design and Designing Research," *Design Issues* 15, no. 2 (1999).

102 Michael Shanks, "Michael Shanks: Nine Archaeological Theses on Design," http://documents.stanford.edu/michaelshanks/260.

103 to Michael Shanks: *all things archaeological*, 2 july, 2014.

104 Jones, *Design Methods*, 4.

105 Cross, *Designerly Ways of Knowing*, 33.

106 Ibid., 34.

107 Glanville, "Researching Design and Designing Research," 88

108 Edward Robbins, *Why Architects Draw* (Cambridge, Mass.; London: MIT Press, 1994), 4.

109 Kees Dorst and Judith Dijkhuis, "Comparing Paradigms for Describing Design Activity," *Design Studies* 16, no. 2 (1995): 274.

110 Cross, *Designerly Ways of Knowing*, 37.

111 Marco Frascari and William Braham, "On the Mantic Paradigm in Architecture: The Projective Evocation of Future Edifices," *Proceedings of the Association of Collegiate Schools of Architecture Annual Meeting* (1994).

112 Ibid., 265.

113 Ibid.

114 Ibid., 263.

115 Pearson and Shanks, *Theatre/Archaeology*, xi.

116 Lesley McFadyen, "Practice Drawing Writing Object," in *Redrawing Anthropology : Materials, Movements, Lines*, ed. Tim Ingold (Farnham: Ashgate, 2011), 34-35.

117 Alberto Pérez-Gómez and Louise Pelletier, *Architectural Representation and the Perspective Hinge* (Cambridge, Mass.; London: MIT Press, 2000 [1997]), 8.

118 Robin Evans, *The Projective Cast: Architecture and Its Three Geometries* (Cambridge, Mass.: MIT Press, 1995), 109.

119 Jonathan Hill, "Institutions of Architecture," *Offramp: detours and dialogues* 7, no. 1 (2000): 73.

120 *The Illegal Architect* (London: Black Dog, 1998), 46.

121 New Archaeology: "a development in the 1960s aimed at making archaeology more scientific, now more often referred to as Processual Archaeology. It proposed that archaeology should openly state its assumptions and use specific scientific procedures derived from Positivism." Bahn, *The Penguin Archaeology Guide*, 318.

122 Eve Blau, Edward Kaufman, and Robin Evans, *Architecture and Its Image: Four Centuries of Architectural Representation* (Montreal: Centre Canadien d'Architecture, 1989), 21.

123 Marco Frascari, "Models and Drawings: The Invisible Nature of Architecture," in *2nd Annual AHRA International Conference: Models & Drawings: The Invisible Nature of Architecture* (University of Nottingham, UK2005).

124 Maya Hambly, *Drawing Instruments 1580-1980* (London: Sotheby's Publications, 1988).

125 Mario Carpo, ed. *The Digital Turn in Architecture 1992-2012* (Chichester: Wiley, 2012). In fact Carpo credits Peter Eisenman with the coining of this phrase.

126 *The Alphabet and the Algorithm* (Cambridge, Mass. ; London: MIT Press, 2011), ix.

127 Ibid.

128 Peter Eisenman, "Visions Unfolding: Architecture in the Age of Electronic Media," in *The Digital Turn in Architecture 1992-2012*, ed. Mario Carpo (Chichester: Wiley, 2012 [1992]), 16.

129 Practice whose aim is physical construction (usually buildings or parts of buildings) requiring contracts of appointment, which uses standard or bespoke forms of building contract and which needs and seeks to conform to building codes and other statutory building legislation.

130 The term 'undisciplined' is used differently here from Bremner and Rodgers term 'undisciplinarity' which they use to define interdisciplinary work between hitherto unconnected disciplines.

131 Pierre Bourdieu, *Outline of a Theory of Practice*, trans. Richard Nice (Cambridge: Cambridge University Press, 1977), 72.

132 Ibid., 78.

133 Ibid.

134 Pierre Bourdieu and Jean-Claude Passeron, *Reproduction in Education, Society and Culture*, trans. Richard Nice (London: Sage, 1990), 31.

135 Personal correspondence with archaeologists: Lesley McFadyen, Birkbeck, University of London; Lizzy Middleton, Cambridge Archaeological Unit; Lorna Richardson, Institute of Archaeology, UCL; Charlotte Frearson, Institute of Archaeology, UCL;

Julie Cassidy, Northamptonshire County Council; Colleen Morgan, University of California, Berkeley and Sara Perry, University of York.

136 Barry and Born, "Interdisciplinarity: Reconfigurations of the Social and Natural Sciences," 1.

137 Susan M. Dixon, "The Sources and Fortunes of Piranesi's Archaeological Illustrations," in *Tracing Architecture : The Aesthetics of Antiquarianism*, ed. Dana Arnold and Stephen Bending (Oxford: Blackwell, 2003).

138 The word "staffage" can mean "accessories" or "decoration," but in the late eighteenth and early nineteenth-centuries, it was used usually in connection with painting to mean a group of humans or animals whose inclusion sought to animate a visual work: David Gethin John, *Images of Goethe through Schiller's Egmont* (Montreal ; London: McGill-Queen's University Press, 1998), 195. [John's translation of the Brothers' Grimm definition at: Jacob Grimm and Wilhelm Grimm, *Deutsches WöRterbuch* (Leipzig,: S. Hirzel, 1854).]

139 Alessandro Zambelli, "The Undisciplined Drawing," *Buildings* 3, no. 2 (2013).

140 Robert Koldewey, Das Wieder Erstehende Babylon. Die Bisherigen Ergebnisse Der Deutschen Ausgrabungen ... Mit 255 Abbildungen Und Planen, Davon 7 in *Farbigem Lichtdruck* (pp. vii. 328. 1913., 1913).

141 Roberto Cassanelli and Massimiliano David, *Ruins of Ancient Rome: The Drawings of French Architects Who Won the Prix De Rome, 1786-1924* (Los Angeles: J.P. Getty Museum, 2002), 81.

142 See: Francis Darwin, ed. *The Foundations of the Origin of Species: Two Essays Written in 1842 and 1844 by C. Darwin.* (Cambridge:

University Press, 1909). and; Jerry A. Fodor and Massimo Piattelli-Palmarini, What Darwin Got Wrong (London: Profile, 2010).

143 Eldon D. Enger, Frederick C. Ross, and David B. Bailey, *Concepts in Biology,* 13th ed. (New York: McGraw-Hill Higher Education, 2009).

144 All terms which might found in a context recording sheet; M. Parker Pearson and C. Richards, "Ordering the World: Perceptions of Architecture, Space and Time," in *Architecture and Order : Approaches to Social Space*, ed. Michael Parker Pearson and Colin Richards (London: Routledge, 1994).

145 Simon James, "Drawing Inferences: Visual Reconstructions in Theory and Practice," in *The Cultural Life of Images : Visual Representation in Archaeology*, ed. Brian Molyneaux (London ; New York: Routledge, 1997), 30.

146 Alain Schnapp, *The Discovery of the Past: The Origins of Archaeology* (London: British Museum Press, 1996), 30.

147 Bourdieu, *Outline of a Theory of Practice*, 86.

148 Ann B. Butler and William Hodos, *Comparative Vertebrate Neuroanatomy: Evolution and Adaptation*, 2nd ed. (Hoboken, N.J.: Wiley-Liss, 2005), 8.

149 Schnapp, *The Discovery of the Past: The Origins of Archaeology*, 30. writing about Jorge Luis Borges's short story of 1940; Jorge Luis Borges, "Tlön, Uqbar, Orbis Tertius," in *Labyrinths: Selected Stories and Other Writings* (Harmondsworth: Penguin, 1970).

150 Stafford, *Visual Analogy: Consciousness as the Art of Connecting*, 10.

151 Evans, *The Projective Cast: Architecture and Its Three Geometries*, 118.

152 Clifford Geertz, *Local Knowledge : Further Essays in Interpretive Anthropology* (London: Fontana, 1993, 1983), 4.

153 Philip Phillips, "American Archaeology and General Anthropological Theory," *Southwestern Journal of Anthropology* 11, no. 3 (1955): 246-47. Paraphrasing, as he admits, Frederick William Maitland's similar comment regarding the relationship between anthropology and history; Frederic William Maitland, *The Collected Papers of Frederic William Maitland*, ed. H. A. L. Fisher (Cambridge: University Press, 1911), 295.

154 Phillips, "American Archaeology and General Anthropological Theory," 246.

155 Colin Renfrew, "The Great Tradition Versus the Great Divide: Archaeology as Anthropology?," *American Journal of Archaeology* 84, no. 3 (1980).

156 Ibid.

157 Deborah L. Nichols, Rosemary A. Joyce, and Susan D. Gillespie, "Is Archaeology Anthropology?," in *Archaeology Is Anthropology*, ed. Susan D. Gillespie and Deborah L. Nichols (American Anthropological Association, 2003), 3.

158 Chris Gosden, *Anthropology and Archaeology: A Changing Relationship* (London: Routledge, 1999), 9.

159 Society for American Archaeology, "What Is Archaeology?," *Society for American Archaeology*, http://www.saa.org/publicftp/public/educators/03_whatis.html.

160 The name given by Tim Ingold variously to a course, seminars and workshops in the Department of Anthropology at the University of Aberdeen from 2003 until the publishing in 2013 of: Tim Ingold, *Making: Anthropology, Archaeology, Art and Architecture*

(2013).

I attended one of these seminars in March 2008.

161 *Redrawing Anthropology: Materials, Movements, Lines* (Farnham: Ashgate, 2011), 2.

162 Bourdieu, *Outline of a Theory of Practice*, 78.

163 Lévi-Strauss, *The Elementary Structures of Kinship*, 10-11.

164 Ibid., 8.

165 Ibid., 10.

166 Ibid., 8.

167 See for example: Antonia Fraser, *A History of Toys* (London: Spring Books, 1972). or; Anthony Burton, "Design History and the History of Toys: Defining a Discipline for the Bethnal Green Museum of Childhood," *Journal of Design History* 10, no. 1 (1997).

168 See for example: Bernard Rudofsky, *Architecture without Architects: A Short Introduction to Non-Pedigree Architecture* (Albuquerque: University of New Mexico Press, 1964). or; R.W. Brunskill, *Vernacular Architecture: An Illustrated Handbook*, 4th ed. (London: Faber, 2000).

169 Generally translated as 'let the seller beware.' Marco Pistis, "From Caveat Emptor to Caveat Venditor - a Brief History of English Sale of Goods Law," *Mondaq*, http://bit.ly/1LgfJUz.

170 Jacques Derrida, *Writing and Difference*, trans. Alan Bass (London: Routledge, 2001), 351.

171 Ibid., 357.

172 Stafford, *Visual Analogy: Consciousness as the Art of Connecting*, 82.

173 "Paying Attention: The Fine Art and Neuroscience of Visual Awareness," *The Comparison Project*, Drake University, https://

comparisonproject.wordpress.drake.edu.

174 "Barbara Maria Stafford: Bio," Barbara Maria Stafford, http://barbaramariastafford.com/curriculum-vitae-bio.html. Key amongst these are: *Body Criticism: Imaging the Unseen in Enlightenment Art and Medicine* (Cambridge, Mass. ; London: MIT, 1991).; *Artful Science: Enlightenment, Entertainment and the Eclipse of Visual Education* (Cambridge, Mass. ; London: MIT Press, 1994).; *Good Looking: Essays on the Virtue of Images* (Cambridge, Mass. ; London: MIT Press, 1996).; *Visual Analogy: Consciousness as the Art of Connecting*. and; Barbara Maria Stafford and Frances Terpak, *Devices of Wonder: From the World in a Box to Images on a Screen* (Los Angeles, Calif. ; [Great Britain]: Getty Research Institute, 2001).

175 See for example: Andrew Saint, *Architect and Engineer: A Study in Sibling Rivalry* (New Haven, Conn. ; London: Yale University Press, 2008). or; Antoine Picon, *French Architects and Engineers in the Age of Enlightenment* (Cambridge: Cambridge University Press, 1992).

176 Joseph Rykwert, *The Necessity of Artifice : Ideas in Architecture* (London: Academy Editions, 1982), 127.

177 The logical category of abduction which C. S. Peirce described as, "processes of thought capable of producing no conclusion more definite than a conjecture." See too; Charles S. Peirce and Carolyn Eisele, *The New Elements of Mathematics* (The Hague: Mouton [etc], 1976), 319-20. and; Alfred Gell, *Art and Agency: An Anthropological Theory* (Oxford: Clarendon, 1998).

178 *Art and Agency: An Anthropological Theory*, 13.

179 Stafford, *Visual Analogy: Consciousness as the Art of Connecting*, 23-24.

180 Ibid.

181 Ibid.

182 Frascari and Braham, "On the Mantic Paradigm in Architecture:The Projective Evocation of Future Edifices," 262.

183 Marco Frascari, ""Semiotica Ab Edendo,"Taste in Architecture," *Journal of Architectural Education* (1984-) 40, no. 1 (1986): 7.

184 Deleuze and Guattari, *A Thousand Plateaus: Capitalism and Schizophrenia*, xiii.

185 Clark, "Jack Cade at London Stone," 177.

186 Alan Sorrell, *Roman London* (London: B.T. Batsford, 1969).

187 Ibid.

188 Peter Marsden, "The Excavation of a Roman Palace Site in London, 1961-1972," *Transactions of the London and Middlesex Archaeological Society* 26(1975).

189 English Heritage., "Heritage Listing: London Stone," English Heritage, http://list.english-heritage.org.uk/resultsingle.aspx?uid=1286846.

190 *Planning (Listed Buildings and Conservation Areas) Act 1990*. and; *Ancient Monuments and Archaeological Areas Act 1979*.

191 See for example: John Yeomans, "What's Happening with London Stone?," *Londonist* [online] 2012. or; Sean Coughlan, "London's Heart of Stone," BBC, http://news.bbc.co.uk/1/hi/magazine/4997470.stm. and; GVA and Purcell Miller Tritton LLP, "London Stone Relocation: Pps5 Statement," (London2011).

192 Stafford, *Visual Analogy: Consciousness as the Art of Connecting*, 183.

193 M. M. Bakhtin, *The Dialogic Imagination: Four Essays*, ed. M. Holquist, trans. Caryl Emerson (Austin: University of Texas Press,

1981), 84.

194 Ibid.

195 Ibid., 208.

196 Stephanie Meece, "A Bird's Eye View - of a Leopard's Spots. The Çatalhöyük 'Map' and the Development of Cartographic Representation in Prehistory.," *Anatolian Studies* 56(2006).

197 In retrospect it is clear to me that the form of the bands owes much to the graphic quality of Charles Joseph Minard's chart of 1869 describing Napoleon's losses in Russia, mapped against time and temperature, reproduced in; Edward R. Tufte, *The Visual Display of Quantitative Information* (Cheshire, Conn.: Graphics Press, 1983), 41.

198 Allan Pred, "The Choreography of Existence: Comments on Hägerstrand's Time-Geography and Its Usefulness," *Economic Geography* 53, no. 2 (1977).

199 William Forsythe, "Choreographic Objects," in *William Forsythe and the Practice of Choreography: It Starts from Any Point*, ed. Steven Spier (Abingdon: Routledge, 2011), 91.

200 Ibid.

201 John Clark, "London Stone: History and Myth," (Unpublished Draft 2015), 14-16.

202 "Jack Cade at London Stone."

203 Julian Thomas, "On the Ocularcentrism of Archaeology," in *Archaeology and the Politics of Vision in a Post-Modern Context*, ed. Julian Thomas and Vitor Oliveira Jorge (Newcastle upon Tyne: Cambridge Scholars Publishing, 2008).

204 Laurajane Smith, *Uses of Heritage* (London; New York: Routledge, 2006), 6. This term is commonly abbreviated to AHD.

205 Ibid.

206 Ibid.

207 Ibid., 7.

208 Tim Brennan, "The Manoeuvre," *Visual Studies* 25, no. 1 (2010): 81.

209 Phil Smith, "Walking-Based Arts: A Resource for the Guided Tour?," *Scandinavian Journal of Hospitality and Tourism* 13, no. 2 (2013): 105.

210 Ibid., 106.

211 Ibid.

212 For example at: "Abide: interventions and performances to re-enchant idle sites of Ipswich, 2006" or; The Bowthorpe Experiment, 2011. http://www.axisweb.org/p/townleyandbradby/

213 Deirdre Heddon, Carl Lavery, and Phil Smith, *Walking, Writing and Performance: Autobiographical Texts* (Bristol: Intellect Books, 2009).

214 For example: Gail Burton, Serena Korda, and Clare Qualmann, "Walkwalkwalk: An Archaeology of the Familiar and the Forgotten," http://www.walkwalkwalk.org.uk/.

215 Francis Alÿs, "Seven Walks," Artangel, http://www.artangel.org.uk/projects/2005/seven_walks.

216 For example: Janet Cardiff, "The Missing Voice: Case Study B," http://www.cardiffmiller.com/artworks/walks/missing_voice.html.

217 Jane Rendell, "Walking Backwards through Brassai," http://www.janerendell.co.uk/walks/walking-backwards-through-brassai. and: "Walking to Wapping/ Walking through Angels," http://www.janerendell.co.uk/walks/walking-backwards-through-brassai.

218 Smith, "Walking-Based Arts: A Resource for the Guided Tour?," 110.

219 Brennan, "The Manoeuvre," 81.

220 Ibid., 80.

221 Ibid.

222 For example at: "Abide: interventions and performances to re-enchant idle sites of Ipswich, 2006" or; The Bowthorpe Experiment, 2011. http://www.axisweb.org/p/townleyandbradby/

223 Brennan, "The Manoeuvre," 80.

224 Anon., "The Cannon Street Stall-Keeper."

225 John Stow and John Strype, *A Survey of the Cities of London and Westminster : Containing the Original, Antiquity, Increase, Modern Estate and Government of Those Cities* (London ; 1720., 1720), 200.

226 Thomas Pennant, *Some Account of London*, [Another edition.]Third edition. ed. (London, 1793).

227 C. E. Street, *Earthstars: The Visionary Landscape* (London: Hermitage, 2000), 76.

228 Robert Fabyan, *[the Chronicles of Fabyan.] Begin. [Fol. A 1, Preceded by Ten Leaves Containing the Heraldic Frontispiece and the Table,] Prima Pars Cronecarum. For That in the Accomptynge of the Yeres of the Worlde, Etc. End. Thus Endeth the Newe Cronycles of Englande and of Fraunce, Etc. B.L* ([London]: R. Pynson, 1516), 624.

229 Richard [RWM] Williams Morgan, "London Stone, Cannon Street," *Notes and Queries* 2nd Series Vol.5(1858).

230 Mor [Richard Williams Morgan] Merrion, "Stonehenge," ibid. 3rd Series Vol.1(1862): 13.

231 Anon., "London Stone," *Chambers's Journal* 5th Series(1888): 241-42.

232 Coughlan, "London's Heart of Stone".

233 William Blake, Milton. A Poem, Etc. [with Illustrations by W.

Blake.] (pl. 45. W. Blake: [London,] 1804 [1808?]. 1804), 4.

234 Anon., "The Cannon Street Stall-Keeper."

235 B. Lambert, *The History and Survey of London and Its Environs : From the Earliest Period to the Present Time* ([S.l.]: T. Hughes, 1806), 491.

236 John Stow and William John Thoms, *A Survey of London, A survey of London, written in the year 1598*. A new edition, edited by William J. Thoms. ed. (London, 1842 [1598]), 84-85.

237 William Camden and Philemon Holland, *Britain, or, a Chorographicall Description of the Most Flourishing Kingdomes, England, Scotland, and Ireland* ... Written First in Latine by W. Camden ... Translated Newly into English by Philemon Holland ... Finally Revised, Amended, and Enlarged with Sundry Additions, Etc (Londini, 1610), 423.

238 William Stukeley, "Commonplace aBook," ed. Wiltshire Heritage Museum Wiltshire Archaeological and Natural History Society Library, Devizes (1717-), fol.25.

239 Stow and Thoms, *A Survey of London*, 84.

240 Ibid.

241 Vestry Minute Book, St. Swithin's Church, May 13, 1742 in John Edward Price, *A Description of the Roman Tessellated Pavement Found in Bucklersbury : With Observations on Analogous Discoveries* (Westminster: Nichols and Sons, 1870).

242 An Architect, "Letter," *The Gentleman's magazine* 68 Part 2, no. 3 (1798): 765.

243 Stow and Thoms, *A Survey of London*, 84.

244 Henry Glapthorne, "Wit in a Constable [1639]," in *The Plays and Poems of Henry Glapthorne, Now First Collected with Illustrative*

Notes and a Memoir of the Author [by R. H. Shepherd]. L.P, ed. Richard Herne Shepherd (2 vol. J. Pearson: London, 1874), 193.

245 Anon., *The British Apollo, or, Curious Amusements for the Ingenious. To Which Are Added the Most Material Occurrences Foreign and Domestic. Perform'd by a Society of Gentlemen*. [with Indexes to Vol. 1-3.] Vol. 1. No. 1-Vol. 4. No. 20. 13 Feb. 1708-11 May, 1711 (London: J. Mayo, for the Authors, 1708), no.104.

246 William Haughton, *English-Men for My Money; or, a Pleasant Comedy, Called a Woman Will Have Her Will*. [by W. H.] (1616).

247 Thomas Allen and Thomas Wright, *The History and Antiquities of London, Westminster, Southwark and Parts Adjacent. With Engravings*, 5 vols., vol. 3 (London: G. Virtue, 1827), 765.

248 Anon., "The Cannon Street Stall-Keeper."

249 Transcribed by the author from of a photograph of the plaque.

250 Blake, Milton. A Poem, Etc. [with Illustrations by W. Blake.], 4.

251 Anon., "The Cannon Street Stall-Keeper."

252 The Church Commissioners of the Church of England, "Confirmation of a Supplementary Scheme Dealing with the Church of Saint Swithun," (Westminster, London: The Church of England, 1958).

253 Fitzroy Robinson, 25th March 1960.

254 James Orchard Halliwell-Phillipps, *A Treatyse of a Galaunt; with the Maryage of the Fayre Pusell, the Bosse of Byllyngesgate Unto London Stone*. [in Verse.] from the Unique Edition Printed by Wynkyn De Worde. Edited by J. O. H (London, 1860 [1522]), 9.

255 Michael Christopher Emlyn Jones et al., *The Camden Miscellany*. Vol. 24 (London: Offices of the Royal Historical Society,

1972), 201. This translation by John Clark in Clark, "Jack Cade at London Stone," 184.

256 Fabyan, *[the Chronicles of Fabyan.] Begin. [Fol. A 1, Preceded by Ten Leaves Containing the Heraldic Frontispiece and the Table,] Prima Pars Cronecarum. For That in the Accomptynge of the Yeres of the Worlde, Etc. End. Thus Endeth the Newe Cronycles of Englande and of Fraunce, Etc. B.L*, 624.

257 Shakespeare, *The First Part of the Contention: The First Quarto*, 1594.

258 1st Folio.

259 The Worshipful Company of Spectacle Makers, "Minute of 1671 Records," The Worshipful Company of Spectacle Makers, http://www.spectaclemakers.com/contact/index.htm.

260 Blake, Milton. *A Poem, Etc.* [with Illustrations by W. Blake.], 4.

261 Washington Irving, *The Sketch Book of Geoffrey Crayon, Gent.* Second Edition (London: John Murray, 1820), 237-38.

262 Nathaniel Hawthorne, *The English Notebooks, Based Upon the Original Manuscripts in the Pierpont Morgan Library* (New York: Modern Language Association of America, 1941), 289.

263 John Crowne, "The Misery of Civil War [1681]," in *Shakespeare Adaptations from the Restoration : Five Plays*, ed. Barbara A. Murray (Madison [N.J.]: Fairleigh Dickinson University Press, 2005).

264 Clark, "Jack Cade at London Stone," 177.

265 "London Stone: The Stone of Brutus?," (Unpublished2013).

266 Anon., "The Cannon Street Stall-Keeper."

267 See Chronotopic Reconstruction above.

268 Site of Encounter: Must Farm.

269 Timothy Darvill, *The Concise Oxford Dictionary of Archaeology*, 2nd ed. (New York: Oxford University Press, 2008), 251.

270 See for example: Peter Drewett, *Field Archaeology: An Introduction* (London: UCL Press, 1999).; P. A. Tyers, "Potsherd: Atlas of Roman Pottery," http://potsherd.net/atlas/topics/tools. or; Lorna Richardson, "Prescot Street: What Tools Do Archaeologists Use?," L-P Archaeology.

271 Albert C. Smith, *Architectural Model as Machine: A New View of Models from Antiquity to the Present Day* (Oxford: Architectural, 2004), vii.

272 Ibid., xvi.

273 William James, *Pragmatism, The Works of William James* (Cambridge, Mass.: Harvard University Press, 1975 [1907]), 34.

274 Dalibor Vesely, "Architecture and the Conflict of Representation," *AA Files* 8(1985): 24.

275 Ibid.

276 Alessandro Zambelli, "Occlusions of the Operational Sequence: A Coincidental Conversation between Robert Matthew and André Leroi-Gourhan in Six Diagrams," in *Architecture and Anthropology*, ed. Adam Jasper (London: Routledge, 2018).ed. Adam Jasper (London: Routledge, 2018

277 Miles Glendinning, *Modern Architect: The Life and Times of Robert Matthew* (London: RIBA Pub., 2008), back matter.

278 A version of this passage first appeared as the abstract to a longer explanation of the chaîne opératoire in: "Occlusions of the Operational Sequence: A Coincidental Conversation between Robert Matthew and André Leroi-Gourhan in 6 Diagrams," *Architectural*

Theory Review 21, no. 2 (2017).no. 2 (2017

279 Stow and Strype, *A Survey of the Cities of London and Westminster : Containing the Original, Antiquity, Increase, Modern Estate and Government of Those Cities*, 200.

280 Text of a commemorative plaque transcribed in: David Wright, "Church of St. Swithin's London Stone," Geograph, http://www.geograph.org.uk/photo/1031034.

281 Anon., "The Cannon Street Stall-Keeper."

282 England, "Confirmation of a Supplementary Scheme Dealing with the Church of Saint Swithun."

283 Draft, and subsequently unused, text for the current bronze plaque. Unpublished letter from Mr. King, City Engineer to Norman Cook, Keeper at the Guildhall Museum, 16th March 1964, MoL ref: Cook, N. & Merrifield, R., T10 (reproduce by permission of the Museum of London Archives).

284 Heritage., "Heritage Listing: London Stone".

285 Coughlan, "London's Heart of Stone".

286 Anon., "London Stone," Wikipedia, https://en.wikipedia.org/wiki/London_Stone.

287 Kevin Greene, *Archaeology: An Introduction*, Fourth Edition, 4th ed. ed. (London: Routledge, 2002), 116.

288 Darvill, *The Concise Oxford Dictionary of Archaeology*.

289 Most prominently quoted, as here, in; Peter Ackroyd, *London: The Biography* (London: Vintage, 2001), 18. but traced by John Clark as a mischievous fabrication by Welsh cleric Richard Williams in 1862.

290 Clark, "Jack Cade at London Stone," 169.

291 Ibid., 170.

292 Zambelli, "The Undisciplined Drawing."

293 Adrian Chadwick, "Archaeology at the Edge of Chaos: Further Towards Reflexive Excavation Methodologies," *Assemblage*, no. 3 (1998): 7-8.

294 Alessandro Zambelli, "Villa Madama and the Scandalous Practice of Raffaello Sanzio," in *'Looking Before and After': Cultural Exchange and the Inheritance of Ideas c.1200-c.1700* (Christ Church College, University of Oxford 2009).

295 Outlined in: Ingrid D. Rowland, "Raphael, Angelo Colocci, and the Genesis of the Architectural Orders," *The Art Bulletin* 76, no. 1 (1994).

296 This diagram is an on-going project and not depicted in this book.

297 Mary Wollstonecraft Shelley [uncredited in this 1st Edition], *Frankenstein: Or the Modern Prometheus*, 3 vols. (London: Lackington, Hughes, Harding, Mavor, & Jones, 1818).

298 Hugh Lofting, T*he Story of Doctor Dolittle, Being the History of His Peculiar Life at Home and Astonishing Adventures in Foreign Parts* (New York,: Frederick A. Stokes Company, 1920).

299 Mary Brenda Hesse, *Models and Analogies in Science* (pp. 150. Sheed & Ward: London & New York, 1963), 144.

300 Ibid., 28.

301 "Models Versus Paradigms in the Natural Sciences," in *The Use of Models in the Social Sciences*, ed. Lyndhurst Collins (London: Tavistock Publications, 1976), 7.

302 *Models and Analogies in Science*, 4-5.

303 Dedre Gentner, "Structure-Mapping: A Theoretical Framework for Analogy," *Cognitive Science* 7, no. 2 (1983): 161.

304 Hesse, *Models and Analogies in Science*.

305 "On Defining Analogy," *Proceedings of the Aristotelian Society* 60 (1959): 79.

306 Charles S. Peirce, *Pragmatism and Pragmaticism* (Bristol: Thoemmes, 1998), 5:172.

307 John McNabb, "The Lying Stones of Sussex: An Investigation into the Role of the Flint Tools in the Development of the Piltdown Forgery," *Archaeological Journal* 163 (2006): 4.

308 Ibid.

309 Shelley [uncredited in this 1st Edition], *Frankenstein: Or the Modern Prometheus*, 124.

310 Hesse, *Models and Analogies in Science*.

311 Barbara Maria Stafford, *Visual Analogy: Consciousness as the Art of Connecting* (Cambridge, Mass. ; London: MIT Press, 1999), 10.

312 McNabb, "The Lying Stones of Sussex: An Investigation into the Role of the Flint Tools in the Development of the Piltdown Forgery," 1.

313 C Dawson and A. S. Woodward, "On the Discovery of a Palaeolithic Human Skull and Mandible in a Flint-Bearing Gravel Overlying the Wealden (Hastings Beds) at Piltdown, Fletching (Sussex)," *Quarterly Journal of the Geological Society* 69, no. March (1913): 147.

314 J. S. Weiner, *The Piltdown Forgery*, 50th anniversary ed. (Oxford: Oxford University Press, 2003), vii.

315 Dawson and Woodward, "On the Discovery of a Palaeolithic Human Skull and Mandible in a Flint-Bearing Gravel Overlying the Wealden (Hastings Beds) at Piltdown, Fletching (Sussex)," 147.

316 Although there is a suggestion with the Pushmi-pullyu that only one head functions at a time; "He only sleeps with one head at a time, you see – very handy – the other heads stays awake all night." Hugh Lofting, *The Voyages of Doctor Dolittle* (New York,: Fred superscript k A. Stokes co., 1922), 61-62.

317 Robert Graves, *The Greek Myths* Volume 2 ([S.l.]: Penguin Books, 1955), 134.

318 Hesiod, *Hesiod, the Homeric Hymns and Homerica* ([S.l.]: Heinemann, 1914), line 300.

319 Homer et al., *The Iliad*, [Rev. ed.] / revised and updated by Peter Jones with D.C.H. Rieu / edited with an introduction and notes by Peter Jones. ed. (London: Penguin, 2003), 95.

320 Hesse, *Models and Analogies in Science.*

321 "On Defining Analogy," 79.

322 Ibid., 80.

323 Ibid.

324 Raymond Williams, *Marxism and Literature* (Oxford: Oxford University Press, 1977); Pierre Bourdieu, *Outline of a Theory of Practice*, trans. Richard Nice (Cambridge: Cambridge University Press, 1977).

325 Masaomi Kobayashi, "The Pursuit of Interdisciplinarities: A Critique of Cultural Studies," in *University of the Ryukyus Repository* (University of the Ryukyus, 2006), 171.

326 For general analyses of these ideas see: Arthur O. Lovejoy, *The Great Chain of Being: A Study of the History of an Idea* (Somerset, N.J.: Transaction, 2009). and; Edward P. Mahoney, "Lovejoy and the Hierarchy of Being," *Journal of the History of Ideas* 48, no. 2 (1987).

327 Williams, *Marxism and Literature*, 106.

328 Stafford, *Visual Analogy: Consciousness as the Art of*

Connecting, 82.

329 Jacques Lacan, *Anxiety: The Seminar of Jacques Lacan, Book X* (Cambridge: Polity Press, 2014), 96-97.

330 Gilles Deleuze and Félix Guattari, *A Thousand Plateaus: Capitalism and Schizophrenia* (London: Athlone, 1988), 475-76.

331 Ludwig Wittgenstein, *Philosophical Investigations*, 2nd ed. ed. (Oxford : Blackwell, 1958 (1997 [printing]), 1958), 67 p.32.

332 Gilles Deleuze and Félix Guattari, "1440: The Smooth and the Striated," in *A Thousand Plateaus: Capitalism and Schizophrenia* (London: Athlone, 1988).

333 Letter from Chris Costelloe of the Victorian Society Chris Costelloe, "Re: Relocation of London Stone (Grade Ii*, Uncertain Date, C19 Iron Grille) from 111 Cannon Street to the Walbrook Building," (The Victorian Society, 2011).

334 Sharon Macdonald, *A Companion to Museum Studies* (Chicester: Wiley-Blackwell, 2011), 8.

335 Letter from Kathy Clark of the Victorian Society to Michael Blamires, City of London Department of the Built Environment: Kathy Clark, "111 Cannon Street, Repositioning of the London Stone (Grade 2*, Origins Unknown, 19th Century Grille and Plaque)," (The Victorian Society, 2013). A more recent application has taken these objections into consideration and advocates the retention of the grille. See: http://bit.ly/1PET58H

336 ibid.

337 Credit goes to Dr. Emma Cheatle for this observation whilst on the Moves of London Stone tour.

338 Peirce, *Pragmatism and Pragmaticism*, 5:171.

339 Mark Cousins, "Building an Architect," in *Occupying*

Architecture: Between the Architect and the User, ed. Jonathan Hill (London: Routledge, 1998).

340 Blaze O'Connor, "Dust and Debitage: An Archaeology of Francis Bacon's Studio," in *Archaeologies of Art: Papers from the Sixth World Archaeological Congress* (University College Dublin: UCD Scholarcast, 2008), 3.

341 Mark Knight, "Must Farm: Must Read," (Cambridge: Cambridge Archaeological Unit, 2012), 12.

342 Ibid., 5.

343 Ibid., 3.

344 Ibid., 4.

345 Matt Lemke, "Give Me Whs or Give Me Death!," *Assemblage*, no. 2 (1997).

346 Ibid.

347 Charles Goodwin, "Professional Vision," *American Anthropologist* 96, no. 3 (1994): 610.

348 Post-excavation note.

349 A 'site of encounter' not detailed here but plotted as tack 3 on Figure 1.

350 Lizzy Middleton, personal email communication, 30th November 2012

351 Lizzy Middleton, personal email communication, 20th January 2013

352 Lizzy Middleton, personal email communication, 30th November 2012

353 Lizzy Middleton, personal email communication, 20th January 2013

354 Alessandro Zambelli, personal email communication with

Lizzy Middleton, 24th November 2012

355 Lizzy Middleton, personal email communication, 20th January 2013

356 Lesley McFadyen, personal email communication, 24th January 2013

357 Presented through Google Groups from Southampton University Department of Archaeology.

358 Interesting and innovative architectural analysis has been undertaken at Çatalhöyük. See for example; Serena Love, "Architecture as Material Culture: Building Form and Materiality in the Pre-Pottery Neolithic of Anatolia and Levant," *Journal of Anthropological Archaeology* 32(2013). or; M.Z. Baranski, "Back to Mellaart a Area: Survey on Late Neolithic Architecture," *Çatalhöyük 2013 Archive Report* (2013)., but "Field Team" rosters from between 2003 and 2014 list no one working on architectural issues who holds an architectural qualification or who describes themselves as an architect; Ian Hodder, "Field Team," http://www.catalhoyuk.com/team/.

359 Gilles Deleuze and Félix Guattari, "1440: The Smooth and the Striated," in *A Thousand Plateaus: Capitalism and Schizophrenia* (London: Athlone, 1988), 475.

360 Ibid., 488.

THE PRACTICE OF THEORY AND THE THEORY OF PRACTICE

The Deutsche Nationalbibliothek lists this publication in the Deutsche Nationalbibliografie; detailed bibliographic information is available on the internet at http://dnb.d-nb.de

Scandalous Space: Between architecture and archaeology
Alessandro Zambelli

ISBN: 978-3-88778-562-8
Publication © by Spurbuchverlag 1. print run 2019
Am Eichenhügel 4, 96148 Baunach, Germany

AADR – Art Architecture Design Research publishes research with an emphasis on the relationship between critical theory and creative practice.
AADR Curatorial Editor: Prof Dr Rochus Urban Hinkel, Stockholm and Nuremberg
Production: pth-mediaberatung GmbH, Würzburg
Graphic Design: Moa Sundkvist, Stockholm